PARENTING THROUGH TANTRUMS: 11 WAYS TO BUILD LASTING SUCCESS

A ROADMAP TO PEACEFUL PARENTING
BY MASTERING KIDS' MELTDOWNS

DR PRATIBHAA BORADE

Chennai • Bangalore

CLEVER FOX PUBLISHING
Chennai, India

Published by CLEVER FOX PUBLISHING 2025
Copyright © DR PRATIBHAA BORADE 2025

All Rights Reserved.
ISBN: 978-93-67070-45-1

This book has been published with all reasonable efforts taken to make the material error-free after the consent of the author. No part of this book shall be used, reproduced in any manner whatsoever without written permission from the author, except in the case of brief quotations embodied in critical articles and reviews.

The Author of this book is solely responsible and liable for its content including but not limited to the views, representations, descriptions, statements, information, opinions and references ["Content"]. The Content of this book shall not constitute or be construed or deemed to reflect the opinion or expression of the Publisher or Editor. Neither the Publisher nor Editor endorse or approve the Content of this book or guarantee the reliability, accuracy or completeness of the Content published herein and do not make any representations or warranties of any kind, express or implied, including but not limited to the implied warranties of merchantability, fitness for a particular purpose. The Publisher and Editor shall not be liable whatsoever for any errors, omissions, whether such errors or omissions result from negligence, accident, or any other cause or claims for loss or damages of any kind, including without limitation, indirect or consequential loss or damage arising out of use, inability to use, or about the reliability, accuracy or sufficiency of the information contained in this book.

Dedication

As a pediatrician, this book is dedicated to all my teachers who taught me pediatrics.

Also, to my two wonderful daughters for teaching me patience and resilience — this book wouldn't exist without you.

To my family, especially my parents and my husband, for the love and chaos that inspired and motivated me to write this book.

To all the parents and readers who will be benefited by reading this book.

Finally. the arrival of my lovely grandson, thanks to whom I get the pleasure of parenting-this time grandparenting-and who ultimately inspired me to write this book.

CONTENTS

About the Book .... *vii*
Epigram .... *ix*
About the Author: Dr Pratibhaa .... *xi*
Introduction .... *xvii*
Description .... *xxiii*

1. Understanding Tantrums: the Hidden Language of Emotions 1
2. Different Faces of Tantrums and Their Types 19
3. The Tantrum Cycle 31
4. Setting the Stage—Proactive Approaches to Tantrum Prevention 37
5. In the Moment: Effective Ways for Managing Tantrums 59
6. Gender Differences and Parental Responses to Tantrums 69
7. How to Remain Calm When Your Child Explodes 81
8. Reconnecting With Your Child Following a Meltdown Storm 89

9. The Emotional Toolkit—Building Emotional Resilience 97
10. Tantrums in Public: Managing Meltdowns on the Go.. 109
11. When Tantrums Escalate: When to Seek Help in Parenting. 117

Short Stories *125*
What Readers Say! *133*

ABOUT THE BOOK

Parenting Through Tantrums: 11 Ways to Build Lasting Success

This book will help you:

1) Truly Understand Tantrums – You will learn what tantrums are and why children have them, allowing you to approach them with tolerance and empathy.
2) Recognize the many types of tantrums – You will comprehend the distinction between outbursts and manipulative tantrums.
3) Understand the Tantrum Cycle: Learn about the stages of a tantrum so you can tell when it is building up, peaking, or fading. Prevent Tantrums Before They Begin to Discover proactive strategies to prevent tantrums and make your child feel understood and supported.
4) Discover how to prevent tantrums – You will discover proactive strategies for avoiding tantrums before they occur, which can also help prevent future tantrums.

5) Currently, effective techniques are used to manage tantrums and maintain a tranquil household atmosphere.
6) Gender discrepancies and parental responses to tantrums.
7) How to remain calm when your youngster explodes.
8) Reconnecting with your child during a breakdown storm.
9) Overview of the Emotional Toolkit for Building Emotional Resilience.
10) Tantrums in public: Managing meltdowns on the go.
11) Know When to Seek Professional Help – Identify the indicators that a more profound issue is causing the tantrums and when it is advisable to speak with a specialist.

With these 11 simple steps, you will build confidence in handling tantrums calmly, connect more intimately with your child, and create a more serene home environment. Whether at home or in public, you will have the tools to help your child navigate their emotions and discover joy in parenting, increasing your and your child's emotional resilience and bonding.

EPIGRAM

"Through storms of tears and tempests wild,
Patience and love tame the child.
With wisdom's touch and hearts steadfast,
Build success in parenting that lasts."

"In the fire of tantrums, strength is born,
Guiding through chaos till calm adorns.
A parent's love, both firm and vast,
Builds a bond designed to last."

"Success in parenting isn't swift,
It's the quiet patience we gently lift.
Through every tantrum's fiery blast,
We shape a love that forever lasts."

"Tantrums roar, emotions sway,
But steadfast hearts will find the way.
Parenting's success, a journey vast,
Is built with love that's meant to last."

Epigram

"With steady hearts and guiding hands,
Through tantrum storms, a parent stands.
Each lesson taught, each trial passed,
We carve a legacy built to last."

"A tantrum's cry, a parent's art,
To calm the storm and teach the heart.
With love's foundation deep and vast,
We craft success that's sure to last."

"Amid the noise of tantrum's rage,
A parent's strength becomes the stage.
Through patience, wisdom, love amassed,
We build a bond that's built to last."

ABOUT THE AUTHOR: DR PRATIBHAA

𝒟r. Pratibhaa is a committed pediatrician with decades of experience in children's health and wellness. She is also an NHCA-certified Child and Adolescent Counselor. She blends her professional knowledge with the wisdom obtained from her parenting experience, having gracefully raised two lovely daughters. With the arrival of her loving grandson, Dr.Pratibhaa has been motivated to offer her views and practical solutions for dealing with one of parenting's most challenging moments: Tantrums.

Her Book, Parenting Through Tantrums, is helpful for parents seeking compassionate and practical strategies to understand and manage their children's emotions during these severe moments. Dr. Pratibhaa's method combines medical knowledge, behavioral research, and her own experiences, resulting in a unique blend of empathy and expertise that parents value. Whether you are a new parent or have children of varying ages, Dr. Pratibhaa's advice in Parenting Through Tantrums is soothing and empowering.

Dr Pratibhaa intends to write more about parenting in the future, having successfully raised two great daughters and enjoyed the adventure of parenting and grandparenting. She plans to write more about parenting in depth with the intention of helping more parents raise emotionally healthier children and better future adults. She also plans to write about positive and loving marital relationships in the future and how can couples maintain the spark forever. The author wants to encourage more people to embark on this beautiful adventure of parenting, appreciate the lovely bonds they form with their children and grandchildren, and build unique lifelong experiences that will aid in developing and shaping young people into magnificent adults with solid life values.

She is committed to creating resources that blend practical advice with imaginative storytelling, empowering parents to foster more profound, magical bonds with their children. This can happen if children thrive in a happy, stress-free environment.

When not writing, Dr. Pratibhaa enjoys spending time with family, exploring nature, and creating new traditions that make everyday moments unique. She believes that parenting is both a science and an art, and we can raise children who thrive through love, patience, and a little creativity. Her books will help parents become the best role models for their children and make parenting a peaceful and enjoyable journey.

PARENTING AND TANTRUMS

ROADMAP TO PEACEFUL PARENTING

INTRODUCTION

"Parenting Through Tantrums", is more than just a book; it is a road map to calm parenting by overcoming children's meltdowns.

This book examines the difficulties of handling tantrums in children through a thorough lens in a very basic and understandable manner. It attempts to provide parents, grandparents, and caregivers with critical information and solutions for navigating the often turbulent waters of childhood outbursts.

Each chapter reviews different features of the tantrums thrown by kids one by one, providing insight into the subtleties of tantrums, so that children can be better understood with empathy. This results in a pleasant, healthy, and nurturing parent-child bond, which will help youngsters become better adults.

Chapter 1: Understanding Tantrums

Tantrums are a regular aspect of childhood development, usually caused by an inability to articulate excessive emotions. Understanding the root causes—dissatisfaction, exhaustion, or overstimulation—is critical for successful management. This chapter dives into children's emotional landscape, assisting parents in understanding that tantrums are frequently the result of unfulfilled demands or sentiments they cannot communicate.

Chapter 2: Types of Tantrums

Not all tantrums are equal. This section categorizes tantrums into three types: frustration-based, attention-seeking, and transition-related. By determining the type of tantrum, parents can modify their responses accordingly.

Chapter 3: The Tantrum Cycle

Tantrums typically follow a predictable pattern: cause, escalation, peak, and resolution. Understanding this cycle enables parents to anticipate and successfully act before a tantrum develops.

Chapter 4: Prevention strategies.

Prevention is essential for lowering the frequency of outbursts. This chapter discusses practical tactics for predicting triggers and establishing an atmosphere that reduces youngsters' frustration. Establishing routines and clear expectations can dramatically reduce the likelihood of outbursts.

Chapter 5: Management Techniques

Having a management strategy is critical when tantrums occur. This section discusses many tactics for dealing with tantrums, such as calming techniques for both parent and child and how to keep composure during these difficult periods.

Chapter 6: Gender Differences

Research shows that boys and girls express their emotions differently, which results in varying tantrum behaviors. This chapter investigates these distinctions and provides ideas for how parents might tailor their approaches based on their child's gender.

Chapter 7: Staying Calm

Keeping calm during a child's tantrum is essential for good management. This section focuses on strategies for parents to regulate their emotions while modeling healthy emotional reactions for their children.

Chapter 8: After the Meltdown

Interactions after a tantrum can substantially impact subsequent conduct. This chapter explains how to interact with children following a meltdown, with an emphasis on communicating feelings and praising positive behaviors.

Chapter 9: Building Emotional Resilience

Teaching children emotional resilience is an ongoing practice that can help prevent future tantrums. Promoting emotional literacy and problem-solving abilities are two strategies for increasing resilience.

Chapter 10: Public Tantrums

Tantrums in public can be very upsetting for parents. This section explains how to address these situations discreetly while respecting the child's dignity and safety.

Chapter 11: Addressing Deeper Issues.

Tantrums can sometimes indicate more serious emotional or behavioral problems. This final chapter advises parents to recognize patterns suggesting underlying issues requiring professional assistance.

"Parenting Through Tantrums" is an excellent resource for parents who want to understand and effectively manage their children's emotional outbursts. The book not only tries to prevent tantrums but also promotes a supportive environment where children may learn to manage their emotions constructively.

Introduction

Understanding Kids Tantrums

Navigating through tantrums can be challenging, but with patience and understanding, we can help our children express their emotions in healthier ways and improve their behavior.

DESCRIPTION

*S*top Stressing About Tantrums - Discover 11 Simple Steps to Understand and Manage Your Child's Emotions with Confidence

Do you ever wonder why tantrums happen and why they are so unpredictable?

Would you like to learn about the different phases of a tantrum and how to deal with them effectively?

Have you ever considered strategies to prevent tantrums before they begin?

Do you wish you could remain calm when your child's emotions flare, particularly in public?

Would understanding how to handle tantrums properly and reconnect with your child afterward be a relief?

Are you aware of how much your child's mental health affects their behavior?

Do you know when tantrums indicate a deeper issue that requires expert assistance?

If you responded YES to any of these questions, this book can help!

Description

11 Key Factors for Parenting Through Tantrums

Dr. Pratibhaa, a physician and NHCA-certified child and adolescent psychologist, walks you through every element of tantrums, from understanding why they occur to responding with empathy and tolerance. This book distils the complexities of tantrums into 11 concrete techniques that make managing them less stressful and more gratifying.

This book can help you:

1) Truly Understand Tantrums - You will learn what tantrums are and why children have them, allowing you to approach them with tolerance and empathy.
2) Recognize the many types of tantrums- You will comprehend the distinction between outbursts and manipulative tantrums.
3) Understand the Tantrum Cycle: Learn about the stages of a tantrum so you can tell when it is building up, peaking, or fading. Prevent Tantrums Before They Begin to Discover proactive strategies to prevent tantrums and make your child feel understood and supported.
4) Discover how to prevent tantrums—You will discover proactive strategies for preventing tantrums before they occur, which can also help prevent future tantrums.

5) Currently, effective techniques are used to manage tantrums and maintain a tranquil household atmosphere.
6) Gender discrepancies and parental responses to tantrums.
7) How to remain calm when your youngster explodes.
8) Reconnecting with your child during a breakdown storm.
9) Overview of the Emotional Toolkit for Building Emotional Resilience.
10) Tantrums in public: Managing meltdowns on the go.
11) Know When to Seek Professional Help—Identify the indicators that a more profound issue is causing the tantrums and when it is advisable to speak with a specialist.

With these 11 simple steps, you will build confidence in handling tantrums calmly, connecting more intimately with your child, and creating a more serene home environment. Whether at home or in public, you will have the tools to help your child navigate their emotions and discover joy in parenting.

Are you ready to easily negotiate tantrums while also developing a strong, positive relationship with your child?

If so, then this book is for you.

A ROADMAP TO PEACEFUL PARENTING

CHAPTER 1

UNDERSTANDING TANTRUMS: THE HIDDEN LANGUAGE OF EMOTIONS

What Are Tantrums?

The Science Behind Tantrums

Many parents say tantrums are spontaneous, unprovoked outbursts caused by seemingly minor frustrations, like forbidding a toy or a disagreement during bedtime . However, tantrums are not random. They are caused by the special biology of a child's developing brain. Tantrums reflect complex physiological and psychological processes still developing in young children. Digging deeper into the science reveals that these violent reactions are the result of an immature brain trying to cope with overwhelming emotions.

Neurological Factors

Amygdala and Hypothalamus:

Children's brains are in a constant state of development, especially the parts responsible for controlling and regulating emotions. Adults, with their mature prefrontal cortex, are better equipped to manage stress, disappointment, and frustration. However, this area is still in the early stages of children's development. As a result, children often lack the emotional skills they need to deal with intense emotions. Understanding these biological components can help caregivers respond to tantrums with more empathy and tolerance, fostering a deeper connection and understanding with their children.

Critical components of a child's brain during a tantrum

Several key areas and processes in a child's brain contribute to why tantrums happen and why they can become so violent for both the child and the adults around them:

The amygdala

The amygdala, a small, almond-shaped area in the brain, acts as an emotional response center and is crucial in initiating the fight-or-flight response. When a child is overwhelmed with anger or fear, the amygdala activates, triggering a strong emotional reaction. This bypasses the logical areas of the brain, making arguing with the child during a tantrum usually pointless. The amygdala essentially 'hijacks' the brain, making rational thinking in stressful situations virtually impossible. Understanding this biological process can help parents respond to tantrums with more empathy and tolerance, knowing that their children's behavior is not a sign of rebellion but an underdeveloped capacity to deal with extreme emotions.

The Hypothalamus

The hypothalamus regulates bodily responses to stress, including heart rate and adrenaline release. When a child feels overwhelmed, the hypothalamus can activate the fight-or-flight response, leading to heightened emotional reactions during tantrums.

Prefrontal Cortex:

The prefrontal cortex, also known as the 'control center' of the brain, is responsible for thinking, self-regulation, and impulse control. However, this brain area is not yet fully mature in children and continues to develop into adulthood. Young children's prefrontal cortex is not yet well equipped to manage strong emotions, making it difficult for them to 'think through' their feelings and self-regulate. Understanding the role of the prefrontal cortex in emotional regulation can help parents respond to tantrums with more patience, knowing that their child's brain is still developing, and they are not yet fully capable of managing their emotions.

Hormonal Surge:

When a tantrum occurs, stress chemicals such as cortisol and adrenaline are released in the child's body, increasing the emotional response. This biochemical stimulation increases the child's emotions, such as anger, frustration, and sadness. Increased stress hormones lead to more tantrums and make it more difficult for children to regain control of their emotions.

Tantrums are a common part of childhood, especially in young children between 1 and 4. They often manifest as emotional outbursts, including crying, screaming, kicking, and breath-holding. Understanding the causes, types, and ways to deal with tantrums can help parents navigate this challenging phase with confidence.

Pathophysiology of Kids' Tantrums

Understanding the pathophysiology of tantrums in children involves examining the neurological and physiological mechanisms contributing to these emotional outbursts. Tantrums are often a normal part of childhood development, particularly in toddlers, and can be influenced by various factors, including brain development, emotional regulation, and environmental triggers. By understanding these causes, parents can feel more prepared and in control when dealing with their child's tantrums.

Mirror Neurons:

Mirror neurons may play a role in how children respond to emotions. These neurons fire when an individual acts and when they observe the same action performed by another. This can influence how children mirror the emotional states of those around them, including their parents.

Why do children have tantrums?

Tantrums are primarily caused by young children's inability to control their emotions. They express their feelings and frustrations through words. Although they strive for independence, they may be unable to control their emotions. They may throw tantrums in the following cases:

Frustration:

Children often feel frustrated when they do not achieve what they want or cannot express their needs clearly.

Emotional Overload:

Strong emotions such as anger, fear, and sadness can overwhelm them and cause an outburst.

Physical Needs:

Hunger, fatigue, and discomfort can also cause tantrums. Children may need more language skills to communicate these needs effectively.

Emotional Overload

Tantrums are often caused by emotional overload. This occurs when toddlers feel too overwhelmed by their emotions and cannot express them appropriately. Young children have limited vocabulary and weak cognitive skills.

Young children have limited vocabulary and underdeveloped cognitive skills, so they cannot express their frustration. When they cannot cope with frustration, despair, and anger, they express it through emotional outbursts. Thus, emotional overload is not due to bad behavior but rather to a child's natural, instinctive reaction when they feel out of control in a world they are only beginning to understand.

Other Factors That Cause Tantrums

In addition to brain development, several other factors can increase the risk of tantrums, making it even more difficult for young children to control their emotions. These factors are often physical demands and environmental stressors that lower a child's tolerance levels, which can lead to a nervous breakdown in seemingly predictable situations:

Lack of sleep:

Even adults need sleep to control their emotions. Lack of sleep can make young children more irritable and less able to cope with frustration as they age. They were sleeping as adults. Fatigue lowers stress tolerance, making you more susceptible to angry outbursts and less able to self-calm down.

Hunger:

Low blood sugar affects your child's mood, energy levels, and patience, making it much more difficult to control their emotions. Without the proper fuel, the body reacts with increased irritability, leading to tantrums.

Overstimulation:

The hectic pace, noise, and new situations can quickly overwhelm a young child's mind. Crowded environments such as shopping malls, noisy restaurants, and bright stores can overwhelm a child's senses and cause overstimulation. When a child's sensory system is overloaded, their ability to regulate emotions is reduced, and a meltdown becomes more likely. Transitions: Young children can have difficulty moving from one activity to the next, especially when enjoying one activity. Transitions require adaptability and a sense of time, something toddlers and preschoolers are still learning. For example, a child who is completely immersed in play may experience intense discomfort when it is time to go home for lunch. This frustration can quickly become a tantrum if your child does not adapt smoothly. It would help if you recognized when they are overstimulated to prevent tantrums and calm your child.

Below are some common signs to look out for, organized by age group:

Signs of overstimulation in newborns and toddlers:

Irritability:

Excessive restlessness or crying.

Physical signs:

Glassy eyes, droopy eyes, or changes in skin color (redness or scars).

Avoidance behaviors:

Covering eyes or avoiding stimulation.

Excited movements:

Jerky movements, clenching of fists, or kicking.

Excessive yawning and hiccups:

Signs of fatigue and stress.

Signs of overstimulation in toddlers and preschoolers:

Emotional outbursts:

Frequent tantrums and crying when overwhelmed.

Inability to communicate emotions:

Difficulty expressing feelings leads to frustration.

Refusal to participate:

Resist activities that are usually enjoyed.

Clinging or detachment: Seeking more attention or withdrawing from social interactions.

Physical signs:

Increased restlessness, difficulty sitting still, or irritability.

Signs of sensory overload in school-age children:

Increased irritability:

Mild frustration caused by minor problems.

Clumsiness:

Accidents due to distraction occur more frequently.

Difficulty concentrating:

Inability to focus on tasks or follow instructions.

Need for attention:

Increased clinginess or need for validation.

Boredom and fatigue:

Expressions of boredom and signs of fatigue.

Time of day:

Tantrums often occur when a child is hungry, tired, or overstimulated (for example, in the late afternoon or just before bedtime).

Developmental stages

Tantrums are typically observed during rapid growth and development periods, such as toddlerhood (ages 1-3) and rebellious periods when children learn to assert their independence.

Transitional moments:

Transitions such as moving from one activity to another (e.g., playtime to mealtime) or experiencing significant life changes (e.g., parental divorce, new sibling) may act as a catalyst.

Social interactions:

Children may become frustrated in situations that require sharing or interaction with peers, especially if they perceive their expectations as unmet.

Unmet expectations:

Young children are often given specific expectations and rely on routines. When these expectations are not met, it can feel like a significant loss. If a child looks forward to a particular story or snack, deviations from that pattern can cause distress.

This is also thanks to children's concrete way of thinking: they do not yet understand flexibility like adults do, so even slight deviations can feel like big disappointments.

Understanding these characteristics can help parents and educators recognize that tantrums are not deliberate acts of rebellion but rather a natural response of young children trying to cope with an often overwhelming reality. When parents consider the biological, emotional, and environmental aspects that contribute to tantrums, they can approach these difficult situations with an attitude that promotes growth, patience, and, most importantly, empathy.

Responding to Tantrums with Empathy

Caregivers who understand the biological, emotional, and situational factors that trigger tantrums can empathize during these difficult times. Tantrums can be viewed as learning opportunities for emotional development rather than unwanted behaviors that must be punished. Remaining calm, providing comfort, acknowledging a child's feelings, and gently guiding them through the moment can help young children gain control over their own emotions over time.

In the long run, responding with empathy and understanding teaches young children that strong emotions are okay and that there are safe ways to express them. This technique promotes healthy parent-child relationships and helps children develop emotional intelligence that will serve them well throughout their lives. Here, we look at the language of emotions hidden during these outbursts.

1. Emotional Development

Expressing Emotions:

Young children are still developing their ability to express their feelings in words. Tantrums often occur when people feel overwhelmed, frustrated, or helpless. They may still need to gain the vocabulary to communicate their needs and feelings effectively.

Range of emotions:

Various emotions, including anger, sadness, fear, and excitement can trigger tantrums. Understanding triggers can help caregivers respond more effectively.

2. Frustration and Control

Desire for Independence:

As children grow up, they often strive for independence. If a child cannot do something independently (such as reaching for a toy or expressing an idea), it can lead to frustration and a tantrum.

Power Struggles:

Tantrums can also stem from a desire to maintain control over a child. If a child feels their autonomy is being challenged, such as being told "no," they may express their discomfort by throwing a tantrum.

3. Overstimulation and sensory overload

Environmental factors:

Loud noises, crowds, and changes in daily life can overwhelm a child's senses and lead to emotional overwhelm that manifest as tantrums. This is especially common in children with sensory processing issues.

Fatigue and hunger: Pay attention to basic physical needs. A tired or hungry child is more likely to have a tantrum. Recognizing these needs can help prevent the spread.

4. Attachment and Security

Comfort Seeking:

Tantrums may indicate that a child needs comfort or encouragement. When a child feels anxious, he may express this through emotional outbursts. He may try to reach out to his caregiver for encouragement and reassurance.

5. Communication Skills

Communication Frustration:

When a child cannot express his thoughts and feelings, tantrums may occur. The child may be trying to communicate needs such as thirst, discomfort, or a desire for attention.

Model appropriate communication:

Teaching children proper ways to express their feelings can help reduce the occurrence of tantrums. This includes teaching them to use simple words and express their needs with gestures.

6. Coping Tips for Parents and Caregivers
Stay Calm:

Staying calm when a tantrum occurs is essential. This helps create a safe space for your child and models appropriate behavior.

Acknowledge emotions:

Acknowledging your child's feelings and letting them know it's okay to be angry or sad helps them feel understood.

Redirect and distract:

Engaging your child in a different activity often helps redirect children's intense emotions into something more manageable.

Set clear expectations:

Clear rules and boundaries help children understand acceptable behavior. Being consistent helps minimize confusion and frustration.

7. Long-term strategies

Teaching emotional competence:

Help: When children recognize and name their emotions, they can better communicate their feelings in the future.

Provide a routine:

Establishing a consistent daily routine gives children a sense of security and predictability, reducing the anxiety that causes tantrums.

Promote problem-solving skills:

Teaching problem-solving skills helps children find solutions to challenges without throwing a tantrum.

Bottom line: When parents understand tantrums as the hidden language of emotions, they can better support their developing children. By identifying the underlying causes of tantrums, parents can help children better manage their emotions and promote emotional intelligence and resilience as they grow.

Tantrums are powerful, often loud, reminders of a child's developing spirit and emotions. While challenging these moments, parents should be like steady anchors in the storm. Parents can guide their children through these intense feelings by remaining calm, offering empathy, and creating safe boundaries, teaching them resilience, patience, and self-regulation.

Remember, tantrums are a natural part of growth—a space where children test their emotions and boundaries. With gentle guidance, we help them learn to navigate their big feelings with grace, building their emotional toolkit for life. In doing so, we offer them discipline, love, and understanding—a foundation upon which their character can flourish. Embrace these moments with patience; each storm will pass, leaving your child a little more robust and secure and your bond a little deeper.

DIFFERENT FACES OF TANTRUMS

MASTERING KIDS' MELTDOWNS

CHAPTER 2

DIFFERENT FACES OF TANTRUMS AND THEIR TYPES

*T*antrums are emotional outbursts that can affect people of any age but are most typically associated with small children. They manifest in various ways and can be classified by their expressions, causes, and settings. Here are some distinct types of tantrums:

1. The classic meltdown

The classic tantrum is characterized by crying, screaming, and physical thrashing. It usually arises when a child is overcome with irritation or fury.

Context: This is common in young children who lack the linguistic ability to convey their emotions. It might happen during transitions, like leaving a playground or when a requested item is denied.

2. The silent tantrum

Instead of loud outbursts, the individual may withdraw, sulk, or refuse to interact with others. This quiet tantrum might be equally severe internally.

Context: This is frequently seen in older children or people who are embarrassed about having a tantrum but still need to express their irritation or disappointment.

3. Manipulative Tantrum

Individuals may use outbursts to manipulate others into fulfilling their desires or use exaggerated emotions to elicit compassion or acquiescence.

Context: This can occur when negotiating for privileges or during an argument. It is common for children to challenge limits.

4. Frustration Tantrum

Tantrums can be triggered by feelings of powerlessness or frustration, leading to disruptive actions such as throwing things or shouting.

Context: Frequently seen when a child is challenged but lacks the necessary abilities to succeed, such as when solving a complex puzzle or chore.

5. The Attention Seeking Tantrum

Tantrums occur when people feel ignored or neglected. They may resort to loud crying or theatrical displays to recover the attention of others around them.

Context: Frequently observed in social situations where a youngster does not receive the attention they seek from parents or classmates.

6. Exhaustion Tantrum

Tantrums occur when individuals are exhausted or overstimulated, causing anger and sobbing that may appear disproportionate to the stimulus.

Context: Common during average interruption, such as travel, or in environments with prolonged activity without rest.

7. The impulsive tantrum

Outbursts are spontaneous and generally triggered by exhilaration, disappointment, or surprise.

Context: It can occur during times of transition, such as a change in plans, and is frequently more spontaneous than planned conduct.

8. Emotional Release

Tantrums can release pent-up emotions. These can be sobbing or expressive crying rather than aggressive behavior.

Context: This might occur during stress or sadness when the individual must digest feelings rather than manipulate or disturb them.

9. Social Tantrum

Social cues, such as peer pressure or societal norms, can trigger emotional outbursts.

Context: Common among teenagers who feel compelled to adhere to group dynamics or vent discontent with societal issues.

Conclusion

Understanding the various types of tantrums is a crucial tool for caregivers and individuals. It equips them with the knowledge to respond correctly, recognize underlying emotions and triggers, and ultimately, develop improved coping skills, emotional intelligence, and more productive communication and behavior control.

Tantrums take on various forms.

Emotional outbursts and manipulative tantrums

Tantrums may look similar on the surface, but they are not always the same. Understanding the underlying reason for a tantrum can allow you to respond more effectively and better support your child's needs and growth. Each type of tantrum requires a unique method to assist your child's emotional development and acquire stronger coping skills. This understanding can give caregivers a sense of confidence and effectiveness in their role.

Emotional outburst

Emotional outbursts occur when a child is overpowered by powerful emotions such as frustration, grief, fear, or rage. Young children lack the vocabulary and emotional management abilities to express their feelings; therefore, they may use sobbing, yelling, or even hitting as a coping strategy. During these times, people may appear disturbed and lost in their pain. These eruptions are typically genuine indications of internal conflict, not attempts to manipulate a circumstance.

When dealing with emotional outbursts, remember that the child is not misbehaving; instead, they are attempting to cope with excessive feelings. They must feel understood and supported to properly navigate the event and acquire appropriate emotional processing skills. If not managed effectively, these emotional outbursts can lead to poor emotional regulation and social skills in the long run. They must feel understood and supported to properly navigate the event and acquire appropriate emotional processing skills.

How to Respond:

In an emotional tantrum, your primary priority should be to calm your child down. Start by acknowledging and validating their feelings to help them feel heard and understood. You can say, "I see you are quite agitated right now." It is okay to feel this way. Let us take several deep breaths together to relax. By validating their feelings, you give them a sense of security and show that their emotions are appropriate. This confirmation helps to create a safe environment in which they can reactivate their reasoning brain.

Once they have cooled down, gently encourage them to share their emotions or help them figure out what triggered the outburst. Over time, this enables children to comprehend and express their feelings verbally, boosting emotional intelligence and decreasing the frequency of emotional outbursts.

Manipulative tantrums

Manipulative tantrums differ from emotional outbursts in that they are often planned responses rather than genuine expressions of powerful emotions. These tantrums occur when a child realizes they can use a meltdown to influence a situation or attain their goals, mainly if it has previously worked. Manipulative tantrums are typically sparked when a child has a specific goal, such as wanting a toy, snack, or attention, and they have realized that causing a scene can sway a parent's decision.

These tantrums can be more persistent if the child has already been "rewarded" for their behavior. However, the underlying objective of manipulative tantrums is typically to test limits and discover how much control they have over a particular situation. Parents must handle these situations kindly and consistently to prevent this conduct from continuing.

How to Respond:

When confronted with a manipulative tantrum, establish clear and consistent boundaries. Begin by acknowledging their feelings to show that you appreciate their displeasure, then clearly convey your decision. For example, you could say, "I understand you are unhappy because you cannot have the toy, but crying or yelling will not help the problem. When you are ready to talk about it calmly, I will listen." This reaction expresses empathy while highlighting that their actions will not change the result of the situation.

The idea is to stay calm and resist giving in, as this will reinforce the use of tantrums as a tactic. If you reply consistently over time, the child will learn that this strategy is ineffective, lowering the frequency of manipulative tantrums and increasing good communication.

Example: Navigating a Common Scenario

Assume you are shopping, and your 4-year-old throws a tantrum every time you pass the toy area, demanding a toy. The first time this happened, you gave them a small toy to calm their weeping, assuming it was a one-time thing. However, your child has since learned that throwing a tantrum earns a reward, and every trip to the store now ends with a similar outburst.

It is vital in this instance to stay tough and not give up, even if it is difficult at first. Before entering the store, gently explain to your child that tantrums will not change the outcome and that if they want to discuss something, they must do so calmly. The next time they make a fuss, reinforce your boundaries and stay calm, reminding them that crying or yelling will not affect your decision. Over time, consistent reinforcement will make them recognize that this action will not have the desired outcome.

Here are some frequent forms of tantrums, along with their characteristics and possible causes:

Forms of Tantrums

The Swan That Is Dying

The youngster thrashes and wriggles during this dramatic outburst, frequently followed by loud sobs. The child's strong emotions are displayed in what looks like a theatrical performance.

The Bolt

This tantrum, characterized by an abrupt attempt at escape, occurs when a child gets frustrated and flees the circumstance.

Quiet Protest

The child of this type may sit still, frequently staring and crossing their arms, refusing to interact vocally. Parents may find this nonverbal form of disobedience incredibly upsetting.

The Plank

This occurs when a child protests being told what to do by lying stubbornly on the floor, frequently in an awkward position.

Hide and Seek

Some kids hide or crawl under furniture to vent their irritation or get attention when disappointed.

Roll, Drop, and Stop

This tantrum, a more disorderly variation of falling to the ground, involves writhing or rolling around in reaction to intense feelings.

Shakespeare's Tragedy

This blends several aspects of tantrums into a big emotional outburst, including tears and intense gestures that may seem exaggerated.

The tantrum of "Thank God That is Not My Child."

This type is self-explanatory and captures a moment of relief for parents who do not have to cope with such conduct themselves.

Other Types

In addition to these distinct kinds, tantrums can also be grouped according to the things that cause them:

Attention-seeking tantrums occur when children feel neglected or seek more engagement from their parents.

Frustration tantrums occur when youngsters struggle with jobs or regulations they do not grasp.

Fatigue tantrums can occur when a youngster is weary or hungry, resulting in angry outbursts.

Control tantrums are caused by children's need for autonomy and a sense of powerlessness when denied choices .

Conclusion

Recognizing the type of tantrum can help parents address the underlying needs or emotions behind the behavior. Understanding that these outbursts are typically a child's way of expressing unmet needs, whether bodily (hunger, weariness) or emotional (frustration, want for attention), can help you manage these complex situations more successfully.

Final Thoughts On Tantrums

Understanding the difference between emotional and manipulative tantrums allows you to respond in ways that support your child's emotional development and independence. Providing empathy and calm direction during emotional outbursts teaches your child that their feelings are valid and helps them build emotional management skills. Maintaining firm boundaries during manipulative tantrums reinforces positive behavior while discouraging attempts to gain control through meltdowns. In both cases, your approach establishes the framework for good emotional expression and management, which will help your child develop resilience and social skills as they grow older.

TANTRUM CYCLE

- 1 TRIGGER
- 2 BUILD UP
- 3 THE STORM
- 4 DESCENT
- 5 COOL DOWN
- 6 AFTERMATH

CHAPTER 3

THE TANTRUM CYCLE

*U*nderstanding the many stages of a tantrum can help caregivers and parents determine when and how to respond appropriately. Recognizing the usual tantrum cycle allows you to approach each stage with a strategy based on the child's emotional state and needs.

Tantrum phases

The Trigger:

The trigger is the spark that initiates the tantrum. This could be caused by various circumstances, such as being told "no," dealing with unexpected changes, feeling tired or hungry, or experiencing overwhelming sensory stimuli. The trigger may appear minor to an adult, but it can feel enormous to a child. For example, suppose a child is having a lovely time at the park, and it is time to leave. In that case, the abrupt transition might be emotionally charged, even if it is expected. Recognizing triggers is critical because it empowers parents to anticipate potential outbursts and mentally plan how to respond, giving them a sense of control in managing tantrums.

The Buildup

During the buildup phase, the child's irritation grows. This stage might vary in duration and intensity. You may notice tense or fidgety body language and louder or more agitated vocalizations. They may begin to express their rage by whining, crying, or performing physical actions such as stomping their feet. This phase is crucial for caregivers to understand because it helps them intervene before the tantrum peaks. Distraction, redirection, or simply acknowledging their feelings can all be effective methods now. For example, if a child grumbles about leaving the park, presenting a countdown to departure or suggesting a fun activity for later may help ease the transition.

Escalation:

The child's emotions intensify, resulting in more screaming, yelling, or physical acts of dissatisfaction. This is usually when the tantrum reaches its peak intensity.

The Explosion or the Peak:

The explosion marks the culmination of the tantrum when the child's emotional response reaches its peak. The peak stage is when the tantrum is at its most intense. The youngster may be troubled, exhibiting actions such as throwing objects, kicking, and shouting. Children may cry, wail, kick, or throw items during this era. Their actions are driven exclusively by emotion, and rational or logical explanations are unlikely to penetrate their emotional state. Rather than attempting to communicate or reason with them, being calm and giving a safe space for the child to vent their emotions is often more beneficial. This could include allowing them to vent while ensuring they are in a secure environment where they will not endanger themselves or others. Even amid chaos, maintaining a calm presence can help them feel safe.

Descent:

After reaching its climax, the severity of the tantrum begins to decrease. The youngster may start to settle down, although they may still be upset.

The Cool Down:

After the eruption, the child will eventually calm down. They may show signs of exhaustion by moving slowly, making fewer vocalizations, or wanting to cuddle or be held. This stage is crucial for communicating and instructing. It is an excellent time for parents to provide comfort and reassurance, supporting them in understanding their emotions and what occurred. This role of the parent in providing comfort during the cooldown can make the child feel supported and nurtured, aiding in their emotional development.

Consider the following scenario. A child demands dessert before dinner. When you gently say no, they whine (the trigger). As you insist on food first, their irritation escalates, and they begin wailing and howling. They quickly reached the peak of the explosion phase, throwing themselves on the ground and shrieking.

Instead of arguing with them right now, which is unlikely to be constructive, wait till they have calmed down. You can position yourself nearby to provide a reassuring presence, such as a gentle touch, or sit silently to let them know you are there. When children begin the cooldown time, they are more likely to understand why dessert comes after dinner.

Now, you can calmly say, "I understand you really wanted dessert, and disappointment is okay. But dinner is important for our health, and we may indulge in dessert later." This approach acknowledges their emotions and gently enforces boundaries and expectations.

Aftermath:

Following the tantrum, the youngster may experience exhaustion or embarrassment. This is an important phase for parents to educate emotional moderation and talk about what happened. By being proactive in this phase, parents can help their child understand and learn from the tantrum, making them feel prepared for future situations.

Conclusion:

Understanding the tantrum cycle enables parents to approach each phase with empathy and ideas for their child's emotional growth. Recognizing triggers and intervening during the buildup can assist in avoiding the explosion phase while being calm and providing comfort during the cooldown can foster a sense of security and connectedness. Over time, this understanding can lead to more effective communication and a stronger parent-child relationship, promoting emotional resilience in children as they learn to control their feelings and frustrations.

CHAPTER 4

SETTING THE STAGE—PROACTIVE APPROACHES TO TANTRUM PREVENTION

Preventing Tantrums Before They Happen

While it is hard to prevent all tantrums, many meltdowns can be averted by preventive measures. Understanding your child's needs, creating clear expectations, and providing them with tools for emotional regulation are all critical components of tantrum prevention.

Effective Ways to Prevent Tantrums

Preventing tantrums in children involves understanding their needs and emotions, creating a supportive environment, and establishing routines. Here are some effective strategies to help minimize the occurrence of tantrums:

1. Establish a Consistent Routine

Children thrive on predictability. Maintaining a regular schedule for meals, naps, and activities can help your child feel secure and less anxious. This structure reduces the likelihood of tantrums triggered by unexpected changes or transitions.

2. Prioritize Sleep and Nutrition

A well-rested and well-fed child is less prone to tantrums. Ensure your child gets adequate sleep (11-14 hours for toddlers) and regular meals with healthy snacks. Avoid letting them get too hungry, as hunger can lead to irritability and outbursts.

3. Provide Choices

Offering choices throughout the day can empower your child and reduce feelings of frustration. Simple decisions, like choosing between two snacks or picking out clothes, can give them a sense of control and help prevent tantrums.

4. Prepare for Transitions

Give your child advance notice before transitioning from one activity to another. For example, a five-minute warning before ending playtime can help them mentally prepare for the change, making it easier for them to cope.

5. *Model Calm Behavior*

Children learn how to manage their emotions by observing their parents. By staying calm during stressful situations, you teach your child to handle their feelings effectively. Use deep breathing or positive self-talk to maintain your composure.

6. *Redirect Attention*

If you sense a tantrum brewing, redirect your child's focus to another activity or toy. Engaging them in a fun game or introducing an enjoyable distraction can diffuse the situation before it escalates.

7. *Control the Environment*

Be mindful of your child's surroundings and remove potential triggers for tantrums. For instance, if loud noises or overcrowded places upset your child, try to avoid those situations or find quieter alternatives when possible.

8. *Spend Quality Time Together*

Regularly engaging in positive interactions with your child can fulfill their emotional needs and reduce attention-seeking behaviors that may lead to tantrums. Set aside time each day for activities that strengthen your bond.

9. Teach Emotional Vocabulary

Help your child express their feelings by teaching them words to describe their emotions, such as "angry," "sad," or "frustrated." This skill enables them to communicate their needs more effectively instead of resorting to tantrums

10. Ensure Plenty of Physical Activity

Encourage outdoor play and physical activities that allow your child to expend energy positively. Regular exercise can improve mood and reduce stress, which may help prevent tantrums.

By consistently implementing these strategies, parents can create an environment that minimizes the likelihood of tantrums while also fostering emotional development in their children.

Some more Tips To Stop Tantrums Before They Start

How can I identify common triggers for tantrums in my child?

Identifying your child's behavior triggers.

Identifying common triggers for tantrums in your child is essential for effective management and prevention. Here are some strategies to help you pinpoint these triggers:

Setting the Stage—Proactive Approaches to Tantrum Prevention

A. *Keep a Tantrum Log*

Documenting the details surrounding each tantrum can reveal patterns over time. Note the following:

Time of Day: Are tantrums more frequent at specific times, such as before meals or bedtime?

Location: Where do tantrums typically occur? Is it at home, in stores, or during outings?

Presence of Others: Who is around during the tantrum? Are there specific people that may influence your child's behavior?

Activities Before Tantrums: What was your child doing right before the outburst? Were they engaged in a fun activity they didn't want to end?

B. *Monitor Physical Needs*

Common physical triggers include:

Hunger:

Children often become irritable when they are hungry. Ensure regular meals and snacks are part of their routine.

Fatigue:

Lack of sleep can lead to crankiness. Please watch your child's sleep patterns and ensure they get enough rest.

Discomfort:

Check if your child is too hot, cold, or uncomfortable in any way, as this can lead to frustration and tantrums.

C. Be Aware of Overstimulation

Children can quickly become overwhelmed by loud noises, large crowds, or new environments. Watch for signs of overstimulation and consider reducing sensory input when your child becomes agitated.

D. Recognize Emotional Triggers

Emotional needs can also lead to tantrums:

Frustration: If your child struggles with a task or feels challenged, they may react with a tantrum. Observe what tasks or situations provoke frustration.

Desire for Independence: Children often want to assert their independence but may feel thwarted by parental limits. Acknowledge their need for autonomy while setting boundaries.

E. Identify Transition Challenges

Transitions between activities can be difficult for young children. If tantrums occur during these times, consider warning them and preparing them for upcoming changes in routine.

F. Look for Patterns Over Time

By being observant and proactive, you can better understand your child's unique triggers and implement strategies to reduce the frequency and intensity of tantrums.

Common physical triggers for tantrums in children are often linked to their basic needs and environmental factors. Here are some key triggers to be aware of:

1. Hunger

Children can become irritable and prone to tantrums when they are hungry. Even a slight delay in mealtime can lead to frustration, making it essential to keep snacks handy and maintain regular meal times to prevent hunger-induced outbursts.

2. Fatigue

Lack of sleep is a significant trigger for tantrums. Children who miss naps or do not get enough nighttime rest may become cranky and less able to cope with frustrations, leading to emotional outbursts.

3. Overstimulation

Toddlers can quickly become overwhelmed by excessive sensory input, such as loud noises or crowded environments. Overstimulation can lead to feelings of anxiety and frustration, resulting in tantrums when they cannot process their surroundings effectively.

4. Discomfort

Physical discomfort, such as being too hot or cold, wearing uncomfortable clothing, or experiencing illness, can trigger tantrums. Children may not have the words to express their discomfort, leading them to react with frustration instead.

5. Transitions

Moving from one activity to another can be challenging for young children. They often need help need help with changes in routine or the end of a preferred activity, which can lead to tantrums if they feel unprepared for the transition.

6. Being Cooped Up

Lack of physical activity and outdoor play can contribute to irritability in toddlers. Regular opportunities for active play help them expend energy and reduce the likelihood of tantrums stemming from boredom or restlessness.

7. Attention-Seeking

Children may act out when they feel ignored or overlooked. Providing consistent attention and engagement can help reduce the need for attention-seeking behaviors that lead to tantrums.

By recognizing these common physical triggers, parents can take proactive steps to address their child's needs and minimize the occurrence of tantrums.

What Causes Overstimulation in Kids? -

Recognizing when your child is overstimulated is crucial for preventing tantrums and helping them regain their composure. Here are some common signs to look out for, categorized by age group:

Signs of Overstimulation in Newborns and Infants

Irritability: Babies may become fussy or cry excessively.

Physical Signs: Look for glassy eyes, limpness, or changes in skin color (red or splotchy).

Avoidance Behaviors: Infants might cover their eyes or turn their heads away from stimuli.

Agitated Movements: Jerky movements, clenching fists, or kicking can indicate discomfort.

Excessive Yawning or Hiccups: These can signal fatigue or stress.

Signs of Overstimulation in Toddlers and Preschoolers

Emotional Outbursts: Tantrums or crying spells may increase when they feel overwhelmed.

Inability to Communicate Feelings: They might struggle to articulate their feelings, leading to frustration.

Refusal to Engage: A child may refrain from participating in activities they usually enjoy.

Clinginess or Withdrawal: They might seek more attention from caregivers or withdraw from social interactions.

Physical Signs: Increased restlessness, difficulty sitting still, or crankiness.

Signs of Overstimulation in School-Age Children

Heightened Irritability: They may become easily frustrated by minor challenges.

Clumsiness: Increased accidents like dropping things can occur due to distraction.

Difficulty Concentrating: Trouble focusing on tasks or following directions may arise.

Need for Attention: They might become clingy or require more reassurance than usual.

Boredom and Fatigue: A child may express boredom easily and show signs of tiredness.

General Indicators Across All Ages

Physical Symptoms: Changes in breathing rate, increased heart rate, sweating, or signs of distress can indicate overstimulation.

Behavioral Changes: Sudden shifts in behavior, such as becoming unusually quiet or overly energetic, can signal that a child is overwhelmed.

What to Do If You Suspect Overstimulation

If you notice these signs, consider taking the following steps:

Reduce Stimulation:

Move the child to a quieter environment with less sensory input (e.g., dim lights, soft music).

Provide Comfort:

Offer physical comfort through hugs or gentle touch to help them calm down.

Encourage Quiet Time:

Allow them time to relax and engage in calming activities like reading or music.

Communicate:

Help your child articulate their feelings and reassure them that feeling overwhelmed is OK.

Powerful Sensory Calming Activities

Practical sensory activities can help calm overstimulated children by giving them the necessary sensory input to regulate their emotions. Here are some engaging activities that can be beneficial:

1. Sensory Bins

Creating a sensory bin filled with various textures can provide a calming experience. You can use materials like:

Rice, dried beans, or sand: Children can scoop, pour, and bury small toys or objects within these materials.

Water beads or slime: These offer unique tactile experiences that can be soothing.

2. Play-Dough Activities

Kneading and manipulating play dough is an excellent way for children to engage their senses. You can enhance this activity by:

I am adding calming scents like a lavender essential oil.

They are hiding small objects in the dough for a fun treasure hunt.

3. Tactile Exploration

Set up a tactile box filled with various textured items such as:

Fabric swatches: Include different textures like soft, rough, and silky.

Natural elements: Use pine cones, leaves, or stones for exploration.

4. Calming Music and Movement

Playing soft music while engaging in gentle movements can help soothe an overstimulated child. Consider:

Yoga or stretching: Simple poses can promote relaxation.

Dance parties: Allowing children to express themselves through movement while keeping the music low.

5. Weighted Blankets and Compression

Using weighted blankets can provide deep pressure input, which helps many children feel more grounded and calm. You might also try:

Gentle squeezing or wrapping: For a comforting effect, wrap your child in a soft blanket or use a body sock.

6. Rocking and Swinging

Activities that involve rhythmic movement can be very calming:

Swinging: A gentle swing motion can help regulate sensory input.

Rocking chairs: Rocking back and forth can provide a soothing rhythm.

7. Mindfulness Activities

Introduce mindfulness practices that focus on breathing and awareness:

Deep breathing exercises: Teach your child to take slow, deep breaths.

Guided imagery: Use calming stories that encourage visualization of peaceful scenes.

8. Nature Walks

Spending time outdoors can be incredibly beneficial. Encourage your child to:

Explore different textures in nature (e.g., grass, bark).

Listen to the sounds of nature, which can be calming compared to indoor noises.

9. Artistic Expression

Engaging in creative activities allows children to express their feelings:

Finger painting: Using non-toxic paints encourages tactile exploration.

Scratch-and-sniff painting: Incorporate scents into art projects for multi-sensory experiences.

10. Obstacle Courses

Setting up an indoor or outdoor obstacle course allows children to engage in physical activity while focusing on movement:

Incorporate crawling, jumping, and balancing tasks to help them release energy in a structured way.

Incorporating these sensory activities into your child's routine can help them manage overstimulation effectively while promoting emotional regulation and relaxation.

Proactive measures reduce tantrums and teach youngsters how to manage their emotions. Here are some successful ways to establish emotional well-being, with examples.

Building Emotional Vocabulary

Tantrums are typically caused by children's inability to articulate their feelings. Teaching kids to label their feelings gives them a valuable communication tool without causing meltdowns.

How to Teach Emotions?

Incorporate emotional terminology into your regular encounters. When your youngster is agitated, you might respond, "You are frustrated because the puzzle is not working as it should." They will eventually be able to identify and express their emotions verbally. Using primary and accessible phrases might help them make connections between their linguistic experiences.

Example:

At the playground, if your child becomes upset because another child refuses to share a toy, intervene early by saying, "It appears that you are frustrated because they are not sharing. Let us ask if we can take turns. Giving kids the language to articulate their emotions can frequently prevent a meltdown. Recognize their sentiments when they express them appropriately, for example, "I am proud of you for stating you are sad. It is fine to feel that way."

Emotional Check-Ins:

Regular emotional check-ins are also an excellent method to increase emotional vocabulary. This can be done several times daily, such as during meals or before bed.

Ask your child questions such as "How was your day?" "What made you joyful or sad?" This pattern encourages individuals to express their emotions and fosters a habit of introspection.

Additional Proactive Strategies.

Keep Routines Consistent:

Predictability makes youngsters feel more comfortable, minimizing the chance of emotional outbursts. A consistent routine for meals, playtime, and bedtime fosters a relaxed environment.

Benefits of Routines:

Routines provide children with consistency and security in an unpredictable world.

Expectations: Knowing what to expect helps youngsters regulate their emotions during transitions and changes in the day.

Implementation Tips:

Create visual timetables or charts to outline everyday activities. This will help your child anticipate what will happen next and involve them in the process.

Provide warnings.

Inform your youngster about upcoming adjustments, such as leaving the park or preparing for bedtime. This mentally prepares kids for change, increasing the likelihood that they will accept the move without frustration.

Examples of warnings:

Time Warnings:

Use timers or clocks to indicate that an activity is about to stop. For example, "We have five more minutes to play before it is time to leave."

Verbal cues:

Use regular statements that your child may link with forthcoming transitions, such as "In 10 minutes, we will begin preparing for bed."

Offer Choices:

Limit your youngster's options to give them a sense of control. Instead of stating, "Get dressed," you could offer, "Would you like to wear the blue or red shirt today?" This empowers them and may minimize resistance.

Why Choices Matter:

Empowerment:

Giving children choices promotes independence and encourages them to accept responsibility for their actions.

Reduced Frustration:

Allowing children to make choices gives them a sense of control and reduces their chances of feeling overwhelmed, which can lead to tantrums.

Choice Techniques:

To prevent overloading your toddler, limit their options to two or three.

Encourage decision-making in fun situations, such as what to eat for a snack or which book to read before bedtime.

Teach coping strategies. Provide your youngster with adequate coping techniques to deal with powerful emotions as they arise. This can include breathing techniques, counting to ten, or using a stress ball.

Practical strategies:

Teach your child to take deep breaths when they feel stressed. For example, you may demonstrate this by stating, "Let us take three deep breaths together: in through the nose, out through the mouth."

Incorporate small mindfulness activities into your daily routine. For example, you can remain still and listen to the sounds around you for a minute or two.

Validate their feelings.

Accept your child's feelings when they express them. Let them know that it is acceptable to feel a certain way and that their emotions are valid.

Strategies for Validation:

Use statements like, "I realize you are upset. It is OK to feel that way."

Share your experiences by saying, "I get frustrated when things do not go my way, too."

Applying these proactive strategies may create a supportive atmosphere for your child that reduces tantrums and promotes emotional growth and resilience. Regularly reinforcing these skills can help your child confidently navigate their emotions, resulting in healthier emotional development and a more peaceful family life.

CHAPTER 5

IN THE MOMENT: EFFECTIVE WAYS FOR MANAGING TANTRUMS

Parenting during the peak of tantrums can be challenging, but some strategies can help manage these situations more effectively.

Most importantly, try not to get irritated. You are an adult, and your little one is a child. Tantrums, rage, sobbing, fits, and disorientation are standard components of growing up.

Join your child on her adventure and appreciate each impressive milestone.

It will pass far too quickly.

Children typically have tantrums because they have been trained to do so. Through experience, the child has learned that they can use tantrums to gain control of their environment. They may have seen another child do it and decided to try it themselves. They know the parent will "cave in," and give the youngster whatever they want to end the tantrum. Bad behavior is rewarded.

The remedy is to "unlearn" this behavior by refusing to give in to the child's demands. It will take some time, but the tantrums will end once the child realizes it does not work.

When the child throws another tantrum, explain calmly that screaming will not work and ignore it if possible. If the situation becomes too heated, pick up the youngsters and take them out of the public location.

Positive Parenting Tips for Handling Tantrums

Managing toddler tantrums can be challenging, but positive parenting strategies can help create a supportive environment that encourages emotional regulation and good behavior. Here are some effective techniques to handle tantrums positively:

1. Stay Calm and Composed

Your reaction sets the tone for how your child will respond. Maintaining your composure during a tantrum is a powerful tool that helps your child regain control more quickly. Take deep breaths and, if necessary, step away to collect yourself before addressing the situation. Remember, you are in control of the situation.

2. *Acknowledge and name their Emotions.*

Our toddlers are not yet developed enough to understand or manage all of the emotions they encounter. Their feelings are explosive, and they lack the social, cognitive, and emotional tools to deal with them effectively and appropriately.

Your tiny one is enraged. As you can see, he is not enjoying it. His rage overwhelms him, and he reacts by throwing a full-fledged tantrum and breaking apart right in front of you (and maybe a couple of curious passersby).

First, you should relax and accept that this is a natural stage of your child's growth.

After that, acknowledge the situation and name the emotion for your child so that he can comprehend and remember it the next time he feels the same way.

You may say:

"Oh, you are so mad! You are so enraged that you strike the ground with your hands, yell, and cry. I can tell how unhappy and angry you are. You're feeling frustrated because you can't have what you want right now. That's okay, we all feel like that sometimes."

3. Validate it -

Demonstrate your comprehension without being overly simplistic.

Remember this always:

If it is essential to your child, then it is.

We often see reality and events in our children's lives through our lens.

So, you lost that little stone you discovered on the ground; what is the big deal? It is only a stone. You will find another one!

If she is grieving over a small stone she lost, even if it was the same as billions of others, and it doesn't appear very smart to you, do not dismiss her feelings. If it seems enormous to your youngster, it probably is. You may believe that another boy calling your son a baby is unimportant, but to your son, it could be the worst insult in the world.

Take your child seriously. By doing so, you demonstrate respect for his experience while also validating him as a separate person from yourself.

Always validate their perception of the world around them and the events that occur inside it. It does not matter how you would feel in a comparable circumstance. You are not two, three, or four years old. If it is important to them, it is essential. Period. Validate it. This validation makes them feel understood and respected.

You may say:

I know how bad it feels to be unable to watch another cartoon. You wish you could watch more cartoons, so it is terrible that you cannot do so now.

When you say this, be honest and kind. It is not about telling him something is terrible or horrific; it is about supporting his perception of it being such.

4. *Normalize it.*

Normalize it by showing empathy and understanding. Join your child in their emotional state, letting them know that it's okay to feel the way they do. This can help them feel less alone in their emotions and more understood.

Show your youngster that you understand how painful a given scenario is for him. You can tell him a story about you as a child, his brother or sister, or another small child (perhaps a character from a fairy tale he enjoys).

You may say:

"You know, honey, when I was a little girl, my sister would not allow me to play with her unique school supplies, and I was sad about it! I sobbed and was enraged, just like you are now!"

Provide clear choices and help them manage them. This proactive approach helps your child feel empowered and in control of their emotions.

Find a solution together and propose ideas.

After acknowledging your child's anger and demonstrating that you understand why he/she is upset, it is time to work together to find a solution.

You can ask him/her what he/she wants to do to feel better. If they continue to weep and yell, tell them to "*say it in words*". Tell your child gently that you cannot understand them while they are crying, and ask your child to speak up so that you can help. Be patient and friendly.

If what they ask for is impossible, tell them your answer firmly, and briefly explain why. Then, give them 2-3 options.

You may say:

"It seems fun to doodle on the living room wall, honey, but you can't. However, we could draw on this sizeable yellow paper with exciting bright markers, or if you like, I can get out the playdough and build little animals out of it. What do you think about that?"

5. Give affection and teach.

Recap what happened, praise excellent behavior, and explain why some acts were unacceptable.

After your child has calmed down and the crisis is over, take them into your arms, hold them, and reassure them of your love. Tell your child that they are a good boy/girl and that you love them. Teach them about healthy choices when angry and explain why some of their behaviors were ineffective.

You may say:

"Where is my tiny girl? Come here and let me give you a bear hug and wipe away your tears! Oh, poor floor, how you beat him with your hands! "

Tickle him/her a little and then tell them:

"Look how much better you feel now that we chose to play nice with these beautiful pens! You do not have to lie on the floor the next time you are angry. Just come to Mommy and tell me what happened and how angry you are, and we will try to make things better, okay?"

6. Use Distraction Techniques

Redirecting your child's attention to another activity can prevent or diffuse a tantrum. For instance, if your child is upset about leaving the park, you could suggest playing with a favorite toy or reading a book together.

7. Teach Emotional Intelligence

Use tantrums as teaching moments to help your child label and understand their emotions. Discuss feelings when they are calm, helping them learn how to express themselves verbally instead of through outbursts.

8. Use Time-In Instead of Time-Out

Discuss your child's feelings and appropriate behaviors with them instead of isolating them during a tantrum. This approach fosters connection and understanding rather than punishment.

9. Encourage Independence

Allowing your toddler to make age-appropriate decisions helps build their confidence and self-discipline. This could involve letting them choose between two snacks or deciding which story to read at bedtime.

10. Use a Calm Down Corner:

Create a designated space for your child to calm down when overwhelmed. Include comforting items like a favorite stuffed animal or books.

Conclusion

By applying these favorable parenting techniques, you can effectively manage toddler tantrums while fostering emotional growth and resilience in your child. Consistency, empathy, and patience are critical in guiding children through this challenging developmental stage.

CHAPTER 6

GENDER DIFFERENCES AND PARENTAL RESPONSES TO TANTRUMS

*T*his chapter delves into the crucial topic of gender disparities and parental responses to tantrums, empowering parents with the knowledge they need to manage their children's behavior effectively.

Understanding how boys and girls express their emotions during tantrums is not just critical, but it's also empowering. It equips parents with the knowledge they need to guide their responses and foster healthy emotional regulation in their children.

Anxiety and Anger: It's crucial to understand how societal norms shape boys' and girls' responses to these emotions. This awareness can help parents better guide their children's emotional development.

Tantrums, a typical behavioral issue in children, affect both sexes. Recognizing that they are a normal part of development can provide parents with reassurance and alleviate some of the anxiety associated with managing their children's behavior.

Here's an overview of the significant distinctions between boys and girls with tantrums:

1. Expression of Anger

Boys are more likely to express their emotions overtly during tantrums, including physical outbursts such as striking or throwing objects. Boys may also be more likely to engage in aggressive behavior to vent their frustration or rage.

Girls tend to communicate their feelings more quietly. They may cry or withdraw instead of acting out physically. Girls frequently acquire social cues that urge them to be more emotionally expressive but less aggressive, resulting in various tantrums.

2. Socialization and Correction.

Boys: Boys may be able to vent their displeasure through tantrums. Because boys' aggressive behavior is frequently tolerated in society, they may be corrected for such outbursts more slowly.

Girls are frequently disciplined more quickly for temper tantrums because societal norms teach them to be more collected and emotionally regulated from a young age. This might lead to girls learning to suppress or vent their anger differently.

3. Emotional Issues:

Boys may have higher rates of anxiety-related behaviors, such as aggression or tantrums. They may be admitted for "anger management" more frequently than girls, indicating a propensity to externalize their emotional distress.

Girls may internalize their emotions more, resulting in worry or despair rather than overtly exhibited rage. This distinction can influence how caregivers interpret and respond to tantrums.

4. Developmental differences

Tantrums are a typical part of growth for both boys and girls, especially between the ages of one and three. However, the frequency and intensity of these tantrums can vary depending on individual temperament rather than gender.

Tantrums are less common as youngsters get older and better at managing their emotions. Girls frequently have earlier language development, which can aid in expressing emotions before they escalate into tantrums.

5. Parental responses

It's essential to be aware of how societal expectations can influence our responses to our children's tantrums. For instance, parents may be more inclined to intervene quickly when girls weep or exhibit anguish. At the same time, boys may be given more opportunities to express their displeasure physically.

Understanding these variations allows parents to customize their responses to effectively handle tantrums, ensuring that boys and girls have adequate emotional regulation abilities.

Tantrums are more common in boys than in girls for various reasons, including biological, social, and developmental factors. Here are some crucial points to understand this phenomenon:

1. Biological differences.

Neurological Development: According to research, boys and girls may grow their brains at different rates, particularly in regions associated with emotional regulation. The prefrontal brain, responsible for impulse control and emotional regulation, matures more slowly in males, which can contribute to more frequent emotional outbursts, such as tantrums.

Hormonal Influences: Boys may have higher levels of certain hormones, such as testosterone, which can impact aggression and impulsivity. This hormonal discrepancy could lead to more powerful emotional reactions.

2. Socialization and Gender norms

Cultural Expectations: Boys are frequently expected to be challenging and less emotional. As a result, males may not be encouraged to describe their feelings vocally, causing them to show dissatisfaction through tantrums.

Girls, on the other hand, are frequently taught how to articulate their feelings better.

Parental Responses: Parents' reactions to tantrums may change depending on the child's gender. Boys may be given greater flexibility in expressing anger or annoyance. Still, girls may be chastised more rapidly for identical acts. This variation in parental response may reinforce the frequency of tantrums in males. It's important to note that how parents respond to tantrums can significantly impact their frequency and intensity, regardless of the child's gender.

3. Emotional Regulation Skills.

Coping Mechanisms: Boys frequently have fewer tools for dealing with emotions because of societal standards that discourage vulnerability. A lack of coping techniques can result in more frequent outbursts when they are overwhelmed.

Conversely, girls may be given more excellent emotional expression and regulation instruction at a younger age.

Linguistic Development: Girls often develop linguistic skills earlier than boys, allowing them to express their emotions more effectively. This skill can help females better manage their feelings and lessen the risk of outbursts.

4. Developmental Factors.

Tantrums occur most frequently between the ages of one and four. During this developmental stage, boys and girls experience frustration as they want independence. However, they may exhibit them differently depending on the characteristics mentioned above.

Frustration Tolerance: Boys may have less frustration tolerance due to a mix of developmental traits and socialization practices, leading them to resort to tantrums when presented with problems.

Conclusion

Tantrums are a normal part of childhood development for both boys and girls. However, boys have more of them due to biological variations, socialization practices, and varying emotional management skills. Understanding these aspects can help parents customize their strategies for properly handling tantrums in both genders.

Handling tantrums in boys versus girls requires specialized tactics that account for gender differences in behavior and societal expectations. Here are some personalized techniques based on the most recent discoveries.

Specific Strategies for Boys

Physical Presence: A more physical approach may be more effective when boys have tantrums. Staying close and providing a calm, supporting presence can make them feel safer.

Encourage Independence: Parents may encourage boys to manage their emotions independently earlier in life, mirroring societal standards emphasizing toughness. This may include teaching them self-soothing techniques or coping strategies.

Discipline Focus: Boys may be more likely to emphasize discipline and emotional control, as parents frequently feel obliged to develop resilience and toughness.

Specific Strategies for Girls

Emotional Validation: Girls frequently benefit from extra emotional validation during tantrums. Parents should offer comfort and reassurance while directly acknowledging their children's feelings.

Communication Skills: Helping girls express their emotions through words might be beneficial. Teaching them to communicate their feelings vocally can help to decrease the frustration that causes tantrums.

A caring approach is often advised for girls, emphasizing empathy and understanding rather than discipline. This can include discussing feelings after a tantrum to reinforce learning.

Common Misconceptions.

1. Tantrums are more common among boys.

Myth: Tantrums are considered more common among boys due to their muscular nature.

Tantrums occur equally in boys and girls. According to research, while boys may have more openly aggressive tantrums, girls frequently show dissatisfaction through sobbing or withdrawal, giving the impression that they have fewer tantrums in general.

2. Boys are allowed to have tantrums, but girls are not.

Myth: Boys are more likely to show their anger than girls due to societal conventions.

Fact: While guys may appear to have greater leeway, ladies frequently experience faster reprimand for emotional expressions. This can lead to a situation in which girls internalize their emotions rather than express them overtly, resulting in less evident tantrum behavior.

3. Tantrums Characterize a "Difficult" Child

Myth: Frequent outbursts indicate a child's temperament or behavioral issues.

Tantrums are a natural aspect of child development, signaling unfulfilled needs or frustration rather than a negative attitude. Tantrums can occur in all children, regardless of gender, as they learn to regulate their emotions.

4. Tantrums are manipulative behaviors.

Myth: Children's tantrums are seen as a form of resistance or manipulation.

Tantrums are often a child's nonverbal expression of emotions. They are caused by frustration and an inability to cope with overwhelming emotions rather than deliberate manipulation.

5. Boys should be disciplined more harshly for tantrums.

Myth: Boys' outbursts require more authoritarian discipline to develop control and toughness.

Understanding and assistance during tantrums is beneficial for both boys and girls. Punishing children for expressing emotions does not teach them how to control them properly and can worsen the situation.

6. Girls' tantrums are less severe.

Myth:

Girls' emotional expressions are less severe or intense than boys.

Tantrums can vary in severity between persons and genders. Girls may express their frustrations differently, but more is needed to minimize the gravity of their sentiments or the importance of proper answers from caregivers.

Conclusion

Parental responses to tantrums in boys and girls can differ depending on societal expectations and gender norms, influencing how parents manage these problematic behaviors. While tactics may vary significantly depending on gender, being calm, recognizing feelings, and setting limits are essential for all children. Understanding these distinctions can assist parents in adequately tailoring their tactics while developing their children's emotional regulation skills.

Understanding the myths regarding tantrums in boys and girls is critical for effective parenting and caregiving. Recognizing that tantrums are a normal developmental stage and not a reflection of a child's personality enables parents to respond with empathy and appropriate tactics, promoting emotional growth in all children.

AFTER THE STORM

- Toddler scream & tantrums
- Trying & touching everything
- Hitting & Biting
- Easily losing focus

CHAPTER 7

HOW TO REMAIN CALM WHEN YOUR CHILD EXPLODES

Importance of Parental Regulation

When your child has a tantrum, it may appear like the world is spinning out of control. Your capacity to remain calm is crucial for your own and your child's emotional development. Children often seek their parents for assistance in regulating their emotions and maintaining a calm demeanor, which teaches them important emotional management skills.

Being calm in the presence of a child's pain does not imply suppressing your emotions. Instead, you must recognize your feelings and choose how to respond. Children are observant and can see when their parents are stressed or overburdened. A consistent, quiet presence might give them the reassurance they need to deal with their emotions.

Self-Regulation Techniques

Breathing exercises:

Why does it work? Deep breathing triggers the body's relaxation response, which helps to reduce the physiological impacts of stress. When you breathe deeply, your body absorbs more oxygen, which boosts your mood and alleviates worry.

1. To practice, select a comfortable position, whether sitting or standing.
2. Allow your stomach to rise by gently inhaling through your nose for four counts.
3. Hold your breath for another count of four.
4. Exhale slowly through your lips for four counts, releasing any tension.
5. Repeat the process three to five times or until you feel calmer.

Positive self-talk:

Why It Works: The way you communicate to yourself during difficult times affects your emotional condition. Positive self-talk helps to reframe the issue and boosts resilience.

How To Implement:

Make a list of affirmations that speak to you, like "This will pass," or "I am capable of handling this."

When you feel overwhelmed, say these affirmations aloud or in your mind.

When negative thoughts arise, such as "I cannot take this anymore," replace them with positive affirmations.

Take some time to rest.

Why does it work? Stepping away allows you to reset your emotions and acquire perspective. It is not a sign of weakness; rather, it indicates that you are concerned about the emotional well-being of both yourself and your child.

How to apply this technique:

Excuse yourself and move into another room or outside for some fresh air.

Use this time to practice basic grounding, such as evaluating your surroundings or focusing on your senses.

Set a timer for a few minutes to remind yourself to return with a clean mind.

Example Scenario

Consider this scenario. You are making supper when your youngster bursts into tears and requests a snack. As the time ticks and dinner is still not ready, you can feel the anxiety build. Instead of reacting with frustration, follow the steps below:

Take a moment to breathe:

Please take a deep breath in when your child expresses their want. Inhale for four counts, hold, then exhale. The initial pause enables deliberate reactions. Tell yourself calmly, "I can do this." My child is dealing with their emotions, and I can help them. This affirmation supports your talent for staying calm.

Engage your child:

Instead of dismissing their request, consider their emotions. You might say, "I see you are hungry right now, and that is fine. Dinner will be ready shortly. Do you want to help me set the table or pick out a colorful plate for dinner?"

Redirect:

Providing a distraction satisfies their immediate need while engaging them positively, moving the emphasis from dissatisfaction to involvement. This can lower the severity of their emotional response, making you feel closer.

Reflect after the incident:

After things have calmed down, take time to consider the issue. Consider what went well and what could be improved next time. Recognizing your efforts helps you grow as a parent and builds emotional resilience.

These daily tactics can help you control your emotions and create a supportive environment where your child feels comfortable expressing themselves. Remember that being calm is a skill that requires practice, so be gentle with yourself as you embark on this path.

Parental Anxiety and Child Development

Long-term effects: Chronic parental worry can impact a child's emotional development and self-regulation skills. Children who grow up in difficult situations may learn to express their emotions through tantrums if their parents do not demonstrate realistic coping techniques.

This can lead to difficulty controlling emotions later in life.

Mindset Tips

Accept the situation.

Understand that tantrums are a natural part of the growing process and do not reflect your parenting skills or your child's personality.

Focus on Your Response:

While you cannot control your child's emotions, you can control how you respond to them.

Stay Grounded:

Visualize yourself as a stable anchor amid your child's tantrum, allowing their feelings to pass without affecting your own.

Conclusion

Calm Presence: It is vital to have a relaxed demeanor throughout eruptions. Parents who manage their anxiety effectively can create a stable emotional environment for their children, allowing them to process their emotions without resorting to tantrums.

Peace after the meltdown

CHAPTER 8

RECONNECTING WITH YOUR CHILD FOLLOWING A MELTDOWN STORM

Reconnecting with your child after a tantrum can be a delicate process. Still, it is critical for restoring emotional balance and building a positive environment.

Here are some tips to assist you rebuild that connection:

1. Allow space:

After a tantrum, your youngster may require time alone to settle down. First, acknowledge his desire for space. This could take longer than a few minutes if necessary.

2. Recognize Emotions:

After the emotional storm has subsided, continue to acknowledge your child's emotions. Let him know that it is OK to be sad or furious. To legitimize his experience, you could say, "I noticed you were pretty angry earlier, and that is fine."

3. Model Calmness:

Set a good example by remaining calm. Taking a deep breath and remaining cool will help you establish a positive tone when you rejoin.

Think about what occurred. Once your youngster has calmed down, gently bring up the topic. Discuss what happened in basic terms, emphasizing feelings rather than actions.

4. Active Listening:

Encourage your youngster to communicate their emotions. Listen without interrupting and demonstrate that what they are going through is significant to you.

5. Whispering:

After your child has calmed down, engage in a pleasant chat with them. Whispering can help establish a relaxed mood and shift the conversation to something lighter or more engaging. This approach relieves tension and promotes connection.

6. Express your emotions briefly:

Speak up when it is acceptable. You can use "you and me" messages to communicate your thoughts. For example, saying, "I was upset when you kicked the table," helps your child grasp the consequences of his behavior without transferring blame.

7. Provide physical comfort for your child:

Physical touch can be quite soothing. Hug him, take his hand, or sit close to him. This physical connection provides the protection and affection that is needed following a distressing situation.

8. Apologize if needed:

It is OK to apologize if you believe you contributed to the problem. This teaches responsibility and demonstrates that everybody makes mistakes.

9. Play:

Play is an essential method for reconnecting. Whether playing with toys, sketching, or walking outside, play helps children freely express themselves in a comfortable setting and reconnect with their emotional state. So, don't be afraid to incorporate play into your reconnection process. It can help both you and your child relax and enjoy each other's company.

10. Patience:

Remember, patience is key. Rebuilding trust and connection takes time. Showing your youngster affection and support daily will help them learn. They may approach you during difficult times. Be patient and understanding, and trust that your efforts will pay off.

Rebuilding trust and connection requires time. Showing your youngster affection and support daily will help them learn. They may approach you during difficult times.

Each child is unique, so adjust your approach to their needs and personalities.

11. Allow time to process feelings:

Remember that children experience emotions differently than adults. They may take some time to share their feelings over the split. Encourage open communication by asking about the experience: "What was that like for you?"

12. Make a plan:

Help them develop strategies for dealing with difficult emotions in the future. This might include breathing exercises, identifying triggers, using a quiet space, etc.

13. Stick to a routine:

Sticking to a familiar routine can provide comfort, ease, and stability after emotional upheaval. Regular meal and bedtime rituals give children a sense of security and remind them that life is returning to normal.

14. Follow up afterwards:

Talk to your child within a few days of the incident to see if he feels understood and supported.

15. Express unconditional love:

Remind your child that you love him regardless of his behavior. This helps to increase security and trust.

16. Model Self-Care:

Finally, remember to model self-care. By taking care of yourself, you're teaching your child the importance of self-care. If you feel overwhelmed, take a deep breath or get some fresh air before returning to your child. This simple act can help you regain your composure and be more present for your child.

Implementing these strategies consistently can help you rebuild trust and connection with your child after a challenging emotional experience, fostering resilience and understanding for each other.

Remember, patience and understanding are critical in times like these. Every child is different, so finding what works best for your child may take time.

BUILDING EMOTIONAL RESILIENCE

CHAPTER 9

THE EMOTIONAL TOOLKIT—BUILDING EMOTIONAL RESILIENCE

Overview:

Emotional intelligence is an effective strategy for minimizing tantrums and increasing resilience. Teaching your child to control their emotions gives them valuable skills for dealing with obstacles and frustrations. This toolbox includes techniques to help your child develop emotional intelligence, allowing them to negotiate difficult situations more quickly and confidently.

Here are some effective strategies to help your child develop emotional regulation skills:

1. Label Emotions.

Naming emotions allows children to understand their feelings better and lowers frustration.

By teaching your child the labels of their feelings, you will enable them to express themselves. Many youngsters act out because they cannot articulate their emotions, so frustration and rage frequently replace peaceful communication. When toddlers learn to recognize and categorize their feelings, they obtain a sense of control and approval.

Use Simple Language: Teach them basic emotions like happy, sad, angry, and scared. For example, you can say, "I see you're upset because you wanted to play longer."

Discuss Emotions in Context: Talk about emotions related to stories or situations they encounter daily. For example, ask how a character in a book might feel.

How to apply:

When your youngster is agitated, acknowledge their emotions: "You are frustrated."

Use essential words and match their body language to demonstrate your listening skills.

Label various emotions over time, including annoyance, disappointment, despair, and excitement.

Consider this scenario: your child has lost their favorite toy.

Respond: "I notice you are sad because you cannot find your toy. It is OK to feel that way. Let us try to find it together."

Labelling emotions allows your child to understand and accept their feelings without becoming overwhelmed.

2. Encourage Problem-Solving

Help your child learn how to approach problems that trigger strong emotions:

Discuss Solutions Together: When they experience frustration (e.g., inability to complete a puzzle), brainstorm alternative strategies.

Use "What-If" Scenarios: Encourage them to think about different outcomes by asking questions like, "What could you do if someone takes your toy?"

Problem-solving helps your child develop resilience because it demonstrates that there are strategies to cope with and manage emotions. When they are furious or frustrated, they realize they have options and tactics.

How to apply:

Guide your youngster through potential solutions: "What do you think we could do to improve this?"

Provide options to make them feel empowered: "Would you like to take a break or try a fresh approach?"

Encourage brainstorming and listen to their solutions, no matter how trivial they may appear.

Example

Example: Your child is frustrated with their inability to construct a stable tower.

Response: "You are frustrated because the blocks are not staying up. Let us take a moment to consider what we could try. We could put the larger blocks at the bottom. What do you think?"

This method not only relieves frustration but also promotes problem-solving and critical thinking.

3. Model Emotional Regulation

Children learn through observation, so modeling emotional resilience can be an excellent teaching method.

Demonstrating how you manage your emotions teaches your child that everyone faces difficulties and that suitable methods exist to deal with these situations. Your replies serve as a template for how kids may respond to their problems in the future.

How to apply:

When you are upset, express your thoughts in a way your youngster may understand, such as, "I am frustrated because I cannot find my keys. I will take a big breath and continue looking."

Demonstrate good coping skills, including deep breathing, taking breaks, and asking for help.

Be transparent about your emotions and emphasize that everyone has them—they are not to be feared or ignored.

Example scenario: You are having a tough day, and your child notices you are sad.

Respond: "I am feeling a little stressed because there is so much to do. I will take deep breaths and concentrate on one task at a time."

Modeling resilience teaches your child that it is OK to experience various emotions and can be managed positively.

4. Praise Emotional Awareness:

Praise your child for recognizing their own emotions. For example, "I am incredibly pleased of you for realizing you were frustrated."

Children learn by observing their parents and caregivers. Demonstrate how to express and manage emotions by:

Verbalizing Your Feelings: Share your emotions openly, such as saying, "I'm feeling a bit stressed because I have a lot to do today." This helps children understand that it's normal to experience a range of emotions.

Discussing Coping Strategies: When you encounter stress or frustration, explain how you cope, like taking deep breaths or walking.

5. Encourage Expression of Feelings

Create an environment where your child feels safe expressing their emotions:

Active Listening: When your child shares their feelings, listen attentively without interruption. Validate their feelings by saying, "It's OK to feel that way."

Artistic Expression: Encourage drawing, painting, or using puppets to express feelings creatively.

6. Teach Coping Strategies

Introduce various techniques for managing strong emotions:

Deep Breathing Exercises: Teach them to take deep breaths by pretending to blow up a balloon or blowing out candles.

Counting: Encourage them to count to ten when they feel overwhelmed.

Physical Activity: Suggest activities like jumping or running in place to release pent-up energy.

7. Establish Routines

Consistent routines provide children with a sense of security and predictability:

Daily Check-ins: Incorporate time each day to discuss feelings and experiences. This can be during meals or before bedtime.

Transition Warnings: Give advance notice before transitions (e.g., moving from playtime to bedtime) to help them prepare emotionally.

8. Role Play and Social Stories

Use role-playing scenarios or social stories to practice emotional responses:

Role Play Different Scenarios: Consider situations that may provoke strong emotions (like losing a game) and discuss appropriate responses.

Read Books About Emotions: Choose stories illustrating characters dealing with various feelings and discuss the outcomes.

9. Create a Calm Down Space

Designate an area in your home where your child can go to calm down when they feel overwhelmed:

Include Comfort Items: Fill this space with calming tools like stuffed animals, books, or sensory items (like stress balls).

Encourage Use of the Space: Remind your child that it's OK to take a break when they need it.

10. Practice Mindfulness Together

Introduce mindfulness activities that promote awareness of thoughts and feelings:

Mindful Breathing: Practice breathing exercises together while focusing on the sensations of breathing.

Nature Walks: Take walks where you observe the environment and discuss what you see and hear.

11. Reinforce Positive Behavior

Acknowledge and praise your child's efforts in managing their emotions:

Positive Reinforcement: When they handle a difficult situation well, praise them for their behavior (e.g., "I'm proud of how you handled that when you lost the game!").

12. Emotion Vocabulary Building

Activity: Introduce a range of emotion words to help children articulate their feelings.

How: Use books, flashcards, or games that focus on different emotions. Encourage your child to express how they feel using specific words (e.g., "happy," "frustrated," and "excited") rather than general terms.

13. Mindfulness Practices

Activity: Engage in mindfulness exercises such as meditation or yoga.

How: Teach simple breathing techniques, like deep belly breathing or "balloon breathing," in which students imagine inflating a balloon as they inhale and deflating it as they exhale. This helps them center themselves during emotional moments.

14. Emotional Charades

Activity: Play charades focusing on emotions.

How: Take turns acting out feelings without words while others guess the emotion portrayed. This helps children recognize and express emotions through body language.

15. Mood Cards

Activity: Use mood cards that depict various facial expressions.

How: Have your child match the cards to corresponding emotions and discuss times they felt that way. Ask questions like, "What made you feel this way?" to encourage reflection and discussion.

16. Art Therapy

Activity: Encourage creative expression through art.

How: Provide materials for drawing or painting and ask your child to create artwork that represents their feelings. Discuss the colors and shapes they use and what emotions they associate with them.

17. Storytelling Sessions

Activity: Read stories that highlight characters' emotions.

How: After reading, discuss how characters felt in different situations and how they managed those feelings. Ask your child how they would feel in similar scenarios.

18. Physical Activity for Energy Release

Activity: Engage in physical activities to help release pent-up energy.

How: Organize games like tag, jumping rope, or simple exercises like dancing or stretching. Physical activity is linked to better emotional regulation.

Encourage Reflection: After an emotional episode, discuss what worked well in managing their feelings and what they could try next time.

By consistently implementing these strategies, you can help your child develop essential emotional regulation skills that will benefit them throughout their lives.

Building emotional intelligence in children takes time and care but offers long-term advantages. Teaching these abilities at a young age gives your child the resilience and emotional awareness to serve them well in adulthood.

Based on my experience, the child learns by seeing what the parent does. Both mother and father. They know how the mother or father reacts to a particular situation, how the parent deals with frustrations, what their thoughts are on how a man or woman must behave, how they treat the child, and how they treat each other. Subconsciously, they always learn by watching. They start acting like the parent. That behavior will continue till they grow up enough to form their thoughts and opinions, after which, if they agree, they comply and do not, they rebel.

So, it is up to both parents to have a safe environment for themselves and their children to voice their opinions, feelings, and frustrations.

Kids often throw tantrums in public.

CHAPTER 10

TANTRUMS IN PUBLIC: MANAGING MELTDOWNS ON THE GO

Strategies for Managing Public Tantrums.

1. Ignore the judgment.

Parents may feel humiliated or under pressure when their children have public meltdowns. Although most people understand that children go through difficult times, it is easy to feel judged when others gaze. Concentrate on your child's immediate needs rather than thinking about how others will react. Remind yourself that every parent goes through these situations; by focusing on your child, you prioritize their well-being over the discomfort of others.

Tip: If you feel self-conscious, take deep breaths and focus on your child.

Imagine a protective bubble enveloping the two of you, blocking out judging stares.

Remember that most people move on quickly, and strangers' opinions have no permanent worth.

2. Create a safe space:

Overcrowding and noise can trigger meltdowns in children. If you are in a busy place, find a quiet corner or a less-crowded area where your child can begin to rest without becoming overstimulated. Moving to a more peaceful setting can help your youngster reset and feel comfortable.

Tip: When visiting a new location, seek out quiet areas. Knowing where to go in a breakdown might help you save time and react calmly when a crisis arises.

3. Exit Strategies:

If a tantrum worsens, it is acceptable to leave the scene. Taking a quick break outside or simply going can be an extremely effective way to help your child (and yourself) recuperate. Taking a break may teach your child that it is acceptable to stop and collect oneself when their emotions get overwhelming. Just a few minutes away can make a huge difference, and if they settle down, you can continue with the activity or leave if it is best for both of you.

Tip: Plan an exit strategy before your outing. If you are in a restaurant, park, or store, plan ahead of time where you can take a little break, such as a restroom, a hallway, or even a spot outside.

Example in action.

Imagine you are in a crowded restaurant, and your toddler becomes upset. The food may be too long, or the setting may be highly stimulating. They suddenly start to howl or scream, and people turn to look at you.

Instead of feeling uncomfortable or attempting to soothe them immediately, take a deep breath and remind yourself to focus on your child's needs, not others' thoughts.

Transfer them away from the table to a quieter area of the restaurant or outside for a few moments to create a temporary "safe space." Acknowledge their emotions calmly ("I see you are frustrated. Let us take a minute outside."

Model a relaxation technique for them, such as taking deep breaths together. This is a helpful way to deal with powerful emotions.

If the meltdown persists, use your escape technique and exit the restaurant entirely. This teaches your child that if their emotions become overwhelming, it is okay to take a break and try again later.

Each behavior shows your child their emotions are real and worth addressing, regardless of the situation. By doing so, you are also teaching children that powerful emotions are not "bad" or anything to be ashamed of; they are simply something we all experience. As they grow, they will realize that taking breaks or requesting space is okay if they feel overwhelmed.

Extra Tips to Avoid Public Tantrums

Discuss any potentially stressful situations with your child ahead of time. Explain where you are going, what to expect, and what you plan to do. Setting expectations can help reduce anxiety and the risk of a meltdown.

Bring Comfort Items:

Small, familiar items, such as a favorite toy, book, or snack, can help calm and distract your child in a strange or crowded situation.

Monitor Triggers:

Notice if your child is unhappy at specific times, such as when they are hungry, tired, or overstimulated. Planning around these triggers and understanding when to provide a brief snack or break will help prevent meltdowns.

Patience and compassion are essential when dealing with meltdowns, as they can be stressful for children and adults.

It is natural to be frustrated but approach the problem with patience and empathy. Recognize that children are still learning how to regulate their emotions.

Celebrate small wins:

Recognize your child's attempts to relax when the event has cooled down. Recognizing children's development, no matter how small, helps them understand that they are gaining essential abilities.

If you notice a youngster throwing a tantrum when their parents are not around, you can take the following steps:

Assess the Situation: Ensure the child's safety. Determine whether the child is in a position to hurt themselves or others.

Approach quietly: If you are comfortable, approach the youngster quietly and kneel at their level. Use a soft tone to assist.

Acknowledge Feelings: Validate the child's emotions by saying, "I see you are upset." This can make them feel understood.

Offer Distraction: If appropriate, try to distract the child by inquiring about a toy or suggesting a game.

Wait It Out: Children sometimes need time to vent their emotions. If they are not reacting to you, give them space while keeping close by.

Seek Help if Necessary: If the tantrum worsens or the youngster cannot settle down, look for nearby adults or staff (such as store personnel) who can aid or locate the parents.

Do not interfere with discipline: Avoid attempting to discipline or chastise the child. It is critical to respect the parenting style of their caregivers.

It is critical to prioritize the child's safety and well-being while being supportive.

Final Thoughts

Public meltdowns are challenging, but they are a frequent part of childhood. By remaining calm and sympathetic during these times, you gain control of the situation and teach your child essential self-regulation skills. These are opportunities for you and your child to learn and grow; with practice, they will become easier to manage over time.

As a parent or guardian, you must guide your child through life. This includes supporting them through challenging emotions. Before going out:

- Make sure your child is rested, fed, and not thirsty. This will prevent sure meltdowns.
- If a tantrum occurs while you are out, take up the child and go.
- If possible, return home.
- If not, find a quiet location away from crowds and keep your child safe while pretending to ignore him.
- When he is calm, explain that your words are far more effective than tantrums.
- Never succumb to a tantrum. You can say no 99 times and yes once.

Your child will only remember that the tantrum was successful once. It would assist if you were not concerned about your children's self-esteem. They need to understand that you have loving, consistent rules and boundaries. It makes children feel safe and valued.

CHAPTER 11

WHEN TANTRUMS ESCALATE: WHEN TO SEEK HELP IN PARENTING.

*T*antrums are a regular aspect of childhood development, and they typically emerge as outbursts of irritation, anger, or emotional overload. While tantrums are to be expected, they can sometimes escalate to the point where more care and intervention are required. Understanding when to seek help can benefit both the child and the parents. Here's an in-depth look at tantrums and the signs that it is time to seek professional help.

Understanding Tantrums.

Tantrums are common in toddlers and preschoolers, often occurring between the ages of one and four. Several things can cause them, including:

- Frustration over communication or tasks
- Tiredness, hunger
- Overstimulation
- Transitions or alterations in routine.
- They are seeking attention or asserting independence.

Normal versus Concerning Tantrums

Most children will have tantrums, although the form and frequency may vary significantly. Here are the significant distinctions:

Frequency: While some tantrums are normal, if your child has numerous tantrums each day, it may suggest more severe difficulties.

Tantrums typically last a few minutes. Extended meltdowns (more than 30 minutes) can be a red indicator.

Tantrums are generally emotional outbursts, but they can cause concern if they develop hostility toward oneself or others or cause property damage.

Response to Calming Measures: If typical calming measures (such as time-outs, talking, or diversion) do not diminish the intensity or frequency of the tantrum, intervention may be necessary.

Signs That It Is Time to Get Professional Help

Parents should seek professional advice if they notice any of the following:

High Emotional Withdrawal:

Tantrums that are followed by excessive withdrawal or indifference in daily activities may indicate an underlying emotional issue.

Regression in Skills:

If the child's behavioral or developmental skills revert (for example, potty training accidents after mastery), it indicates emotional discomfort.

Behavioral disorders:

Ongoing behavior problems, such as excessive defiance or violence outside of tantrums, can be a sign of more extensive behavioral disorders.

Impact on Family Dynamics:

If tantrums cause significant stress within the family, disrupting relationships, routines, or sibling patterns, it may be necessary to seek help.

Parental Exhaustion:

If parents feel overwhelmed, helpless, or continually stressed because of their child's tantrums, seeking expert help can be quite beneficial.

Approaching Professional Help

If you decide it is time to get help, here are some options to consider:

Pediatric Consultation: Consult your child's pediatrician to rule out any physical causes of the tantrums or emotional discomfort.

A child psychologist or therapist can help assess the problem and provide suggestions that are specific to your child's needs.

Parenting Workshops and Support Groups: Participating in support groups might be beneficial. Sharing experiences with other parents might bring consolation and new coping skills.

Behavioral Therapy: Certain therapies, such as cognitive-behavioral therapy (CBT), can assist children in developing more vital coping skills and emotional regulation.

Family Therapy: Including the entire family helps enhance communication and develop relationships while addressing systemic issues.

Conclusion

Tantrums may be a major source of stress for both children and adults, especially if they escalate. Understanding the nature of tantrums, spotting troubling patterns, and knowing when to seek help can help parents better navigate their child's emotional development. Early intervention can enhance outcomes by instilling resilience and emotional intelligence in children as they grow. Finally, asking for help is not a sign of failure but rather a proactive strategy to support a child's emotional well-being.

Conclusion: Your Journey to Mastery.

This book is not intended to eliminate children's meltdowns and tantrums. It is about comprehension, connection, and development. Tantrums can become less frequent, less intense, and more bearable with patience, experience, and the correct tools, all while strengthening your bond with your child. You can use each tantrum to teach your child about emotional resilience. Every parent has experienced the vortex of a child's tantrum. You are not alone in this. It can hit at the most inconvenient times—whether in a crowded grocery store, on a long-awaited family outing, or while trying to relax at home. Tantrums leave parents exhausted, helpless, and often embarrassed, with the overhanging issue of why this is happening and what they can do about it.

This book provides parents with more than simply fast fixes. It provides a comprehensive and empathic approach to understanding, managing, and preventing temper tantrums in young children. This empathic approach is not about fixing your child's behavior, but about understanding and supporting their emotional development. Rather than viewing these outbursts as behavioral issues that must be addressed, this handbook urges you to understand meltdowns as necessary components of a child's emotional development. With the correct tools, tantrums may become opportunities for connection, emotional growth, and resilience.

Parenting through tantrums demystifies the chaos of tantrums by delving deeply into the psychological, emotional, and biological causes of meltdowns. This understanding will empower you, as a parent, to stay calm, maintain control, and guide your children through these overwhelming emotional experiences. In this book, you learn about tantrums, their types, stages, prevention, and public management, and how to identify certain red flags that indicate a professional evaluation that may be needed.

You learn how to respond to meltdowns and, more importantly, how to prevent them from escalating. This knowledge will bring a sense of relief, increasing your and your child's emotional resilience and reducing stress in your parenting journey.

UNDERSTANDING KIDS' TANTRUMS AND SOLUTIONS

Discover effective strategies to help your child manage their emotions during difficult moments and learn.

SHORT STORIES

Some short stories, complete with emotions, to represent various aspects of parenting through tantrums

Story 1: Nervous Breakdown in the Supermarket

While browsing the cereal aisle, Eric saw his favorite sweet and insisted they buy it. Anna, his mother softly told him she already had a healthy breakfast prepared at home and would not purchase candy that day.

Anna felt a surge of frustration but also a pang of guilt for denying her son's request. She knew it was essential to stick to her decision, but it was always challenging. She took a deep breath and tried to focus on the task at hand.

Eric could feel his face turning red. He began shouting and crying hysterically, upsetting the other customers. Anna closed her eyes and breathed deeply. To her credit, she kept her composure and murmured to Eric as she kneeled beside him.

"Eric, I understand your anger. It is frustrating when you cannot get what you want at specific times and places."

Anna's empathetic words resonated with Eric. Feeling understood, she suggested a healthier alternative, and Eric chose a box of his favorite blueberry-flavored oats. His sobbing began to subside. They left the store, both feeling a sense of understanding and connection. Eric was satisfied with his choice, and Anna was relieved she had remained calm, respecting Eric's autonomy in making his own decision.

Story 2: The Bedtime Battle

John felt a mix of exhaustion and empathy. He knew Mia was trying to push her boundaries, but it was hard to keep his cool after a long day. Mia was three years old and ready for bed, and her father, John, was set to face the same conflict again.

Mia wanted to hear one more story, but John knew it was time for her to go to bed. Mia threw a massive rage as John turned off the light that illuminated the room.

"Why can't I stay awake late?" she sulked, burying herself into her warm blanket.

John sighed and breathed slowly, "I realize you want to keep playing, but you must rest to grow bigger and stronger. Tomorrow's bedtime will be extra special, with a new story."

Mia considered her father's proposition for some time. She immediately dried her eyes and nodded, fearing the tale would not be available the next day. John hugged her warmly, feeling a sense of relief and accomplishment. He realized that minor concessions can sometimes work wonders and save the day, reinforcing their bond.

Story 3: Playground Disappointment

Alex, five years old, was keen to play on the high swing at the playground. However, there was already a child swinging happily. Instead of patiently waiting his turn, Alex yelled and stamped his foot, angry and unhappy.

Alex's mother, Susan, appeared a little later. "Alex, I get it. You feel annoyed, and waiting is tough whenever you want something. I get it."

Alex burst into tears, but his face remained red with wrath. "But I want it now," he insisted.

"Could you join me in counting to ten? If the swing remains occupied after the count, I hope you enjoy the slide."

She counted and discovered that nobody was utilizing the swing. Alex approached it quickly and happily. He had learned that there was sometimes a reward for waiting.

Story 4: Painting Tragedy

Sara enjoyed painting. She liked it so much that she attempted to create wonderful artwork. Unfortunately, she splashed water over her piece during her next effort. In her rage, she flung her paintbrush down and exclaimed, "I am the worst painter ever!"

Nobody should be that upset about a painting, but Sara was. Linda, her mother, witnessed the mayhem and mess. She did not complain, however. Instead, she sat with Sara and reassured her. "These things happen; it is all part of the process, dear. Look what I have in my art box! There were additional papers and vivid paints."

Sara snorted and shook her head, amazed. Thanks to her mother, they painted, laughed, and created new masterpieces together. Sara learned that it is alright to make errors and that there is always an option.

These stories are about feelings, understanding, and teamwork in conflict resolution, and they show the difficulties and solutions that children's parents can deal with tantrums.

Story 5: A Special Corner with Soft Pillows, Dolls, and Books

Amy, who is five years old, was nurtured in a very bright town. She had plenty of things to play with. She adored her toys and would throw a major tantrum if things did not go her way. She felt this way on a lovely afternoon when she wanted to play with her blocks, which Leo, her younger sibling, had taken.

Pamela, their mother suggested that they should share.

This comment was intended to soothe the two children, but it was out of strength, as mom reasoned, "Amy was too angry to listen."

"NO! I want them all! I will not share toys!" Amy shouted and beat her feet.

At this moment, it was clear that there was rage. Instead of becoming enraged with Amy, her mother, with her infinite patience, handled the matter gently and directed her daughter to the Calm Down Corner they had built. It was filled with pillows and books.

Amy appeared calmer once they reached the corner. This was the location where people could express their feelings. Her mother told Amy that she could express all of her emotions, but Amy claimed she was still mad.

"Sure," her mother replied enthusiastically.

"That is okay. It is okay to be angry. Let us take some deep breaths together." They inhaled and exhaled together, counting to three.

Amy eventually calmed down and felt lighter.

She returned to her brother, this time willing to play together. They had a good time building the tower and laughing as they went. In her Calm Down Corner, she learned that everything would be fine even if things did not go her way on many occasions.

Story 6: The Power of Choice

Leo was only four years old and had many fantastic ideas. Pretend play was his favorite game. However, his ingenuity occasionally led to disappointment as he sought appropriate objects for his next imagined adventure. One day, he wanted to build a space shuttle, but all the boxes were gone.

Leo stated that he will create his own space shuttle! He was planning to buy a spaceship.

He hurled the sole tiny box in the room and showed it to his mother. He complained, "This is not sufficient."

Leo's mother, with her deep understanding of her son's feelings, walked in and observed her son getting annoyed. "Leo, what is the matter?" she inquired, "I know you have wanted to build a space shuttle for a time! Let us sit and consider possibilities."

Leo sulked, arms folded, but did not dispute. "What are the alternatives?"

His mother, with her wise guidance, said, "You can sit back, relax, and sketch the design of your spaceship, or we can go scavenger hunting for other items in the home."

After a moment, Leo sighed. "All good. We shall look for more materials then."

They searched the house, discovering old pillows, bed sheets, and an orange umbrella. Then, they joyfully worked together to transform their living room into a magnificent spacecraft, their laughter echoing through the house.

Leo, feeling a sense of relief, recovered his composure, and his wrath was completely smothered. Through his decisions, he realized that there are always new opportunities to be explored when one has a positive attitude about failure.

Story 7: The Lost Toy Crisis.

Three-year-old Daniel was at the park when he discovered he had misplaced his favorite dinosaur toy. He was devastated.

He screamed, wailed, and refused to leave until they found him again. From his perspective, he had lost his best friend, his trusted companion, and it was a heartbreaking moment for him.

His mother, Lily, saw this dinosaur's importance to Daniel and approached him gently. She understood that the loss of the toy was not just a trivial matter for Daniel, but a significant emotional event. She said, "I realize it must be difficult for you to part with Dino. I would like us to look for him for a few moments together. If we cannot find anything, I will assist you in making new dinosaur toys when we get home. How does that sound?"

Daniel let out a snort and considered his choices. "Can we make it green?" he said, wiping away tears.

Of course. I will construct a massive green dinosaur. Lisa gladly confirmed that she would.

With this notion, Daniel, showing resilience and understanding, agreed to search for one more location before leaving. Though he did not meet Mr. Dino, he left the park thinking about the new adventures ahead and smiling slowly as the evening fell.

These stories relate parents' accounts of shifted tantrums with empathy, inventiveness, and encouragement, which helps to develop children's resilience and comprehension.

They discuss feelings, understanding, and participation in conflict resolution and the obstacles and strategies parents can use to deal with tantrums.

WHAT READERS SAY!

Top reviews from India

Barkha kadam

5.0 out of 5 stars A Treasure of Wisdom in Improving Emotional Resilience In Kids

Reviewed in India on 9 November 2024

The author takes inferences from real-life as well as practical psychologically based study in coming up with solutions. She reinforces the strategies of calm and effective emotional building methods of parents with their children.

This book offers a spectrum of approaches in strengthening parents' connection with their kids and offer practical wisdom in dealing with emotional resilience.

Kindle Customer

5.0 out of 5 stars Mindful parenting

Reviewed in India on 8 November 2024

Any parent would be eager to get their hands on Dr. Pratibha's work on parenting. Her guidance elevates consciousness and provides practical insights on approaching sensitive topics like children's tantrums. Many thanks for this valuable resource! 💯❤️

One person found this helpful

Vidhaatri

5.0 out of 5 stars An invaluable guide for parent

Reviewed in India on 19 November 2024

"11 Key Factors in Parenting Through Tantrums" is an invaluable guide for any parent struggling with their child's emotional outbursts. Dr. Pratibhaa offers a compassionate and practical roadmap, breaking down tantrums into understandable phases and providing 11 actionable steps to help manage them. I especially appreciated the chapter on preventing tantrums before they even start, and the insightful strategies for staying calm during emotional outbursts, whether at home or in public. This book not only teaches how to manage tantrums but also emphasizes the importance of reconnecting with your child afterward, making it a truly holistic approach to peaceful parenting. A must-read for anyone looking to bring more harmony and understanding into their parenting journey."

Vasu G S

5.0 out of 5 stars A must read for parents!

Reviewed in India on 14 November 2024

Dr. Pratibhaa's Stop Stressing Over Tantrums offers a thoughtful, empathetic, and highly practical approach to one of the most challenging aspects of parenting: managing tantrums. In this accessible guide, the author, a pediatrician and certified child counselor, provides parents with clear, actionable steps to not only understand the underlying causes of tantrums but to respond to them in ways that foster emotional connection and resilience in children.

The book is divided into 11 key steps, each addressing different facets of tantrums, from prevention to effective management and post-tantrum reconnection. The first few chapters are dedicated to understanding the psychology behind tantrums—why they happen, what they signify, and how to recognize the different "faces" they may take, from outbursts to manipulative behaviors. By arming parents with knowledge of the tantrum cycle, Dr. Pratibhaa gives them the tools to anticipate, identify, and de-escalate these emotional episodes before they spiral out of control.

What makes this book particularly valuable is its focus on empathy. Instead of advocating for punitive measures or trying to suppress emotions, the author emphasizes the importance of understanding the child's emotional state and responding with patience and compassion. This not only helps to calm the child during an emotional outburst but also promotes long-term emotional resilience.

A standout feature of the book is its guidance on how to stay calm and composed during tantrums, especially in public settings. For many parents, public meltdowns can be particularly stressful, but Dr. Pratibhaa offers practical tips on how to manage these situations without feeling overwhelmed or embarrassed. Whether at home or in a public place, the book provides reassuring advice for keeping emotions in check and maintaining control.

One of the most helpful chapters addresses what to do after a tantrum. Reconnecting with your child in a positive, reassuring manner after the storm has passed is essential for strengthening the parent-child bond. Dr. Pratibhaa explains how this post-tantrum phase is crucial for emotional healing, offering strategies that promote reconciliation and understanding.

The book also touches on the broader picture of child development, exploring how physical health—such as sleep, diet, and stress—can influence behavior and lead to more frequent tantrums. The insights into how emotional well-being impacts behavior are invaluable for parents looking to provide a holistic approach to their child's needs.

Perhaps one of the most important aspects of the book is its emphasis on recognizing when professional help may be needed. Dr. Pratibhaa offers a clear guide for parents to know when tantrums may be indicative of deeper emotional or behavioral issues that require the intervention of a counselor or therapist.

In conclusion, Stop Stressing Over Tantrums is a must-read for any parent looking for practical, compassionate strategies for managing their child's emotional outbursts. The 11 steps are straightforward yet profound, offering parents the tools to handle tantrums with confidence, empathy, and calmness. With this book.

Top reviews from the United States

Dinesh Rohra

5.0 out of 5 stars Wonderful insights to help toddlers and parents alike!

Reviewed in the United States on November 9, 2024

Must read for toddler parents! This book offers valuable insight into understanding tantrums from a toddler's perspective making it so much easier for young parents.

The author is a pediatrician herself, she has explained the physiological science behind tantrums. Being a toddler parent myself, getting this scientific perspective has really made me more empathetic to my toddler since now I fully understand that his tantrums are not intentional.

Ashutosh Folane

5.0 out of 5 stars Essential guide for every parent

Reviewed in the United States on November 9, 2024

This book offers practical and compassionate advice on managing tantrums, turning a challenging aspect of parenting into an opportunity for growth. The 11 key factors are clearly explained, making it easy to apply the strategies in real-life situations. I especially appreciated the roadmap for staying calm and connected during difficult moments. Highly recommended for anyone looking to build a peaceful and positive parenting approach!

www.ingramcontent.com/pod-product-compliance
Lightning Source LLC
LaVergne TN
LVHW041842070526
838199LV00045BA/1392